SEVEN

TI.

TO

Survival

Overcoming the Speed Bumps
on Your Journey

YOULANDA CUMINGS WASHINGTON

Seven Tips to Survival
Copyright © 2023 by Youlanda Cumings Washington

Printed in the United States of America.

ISBN
979-8-88945-414-4 (Paperback)
979-8-88945-415-1 (eBook)

Brilliant Books Literary
137 Forest Park Lane Thomasville
North Carolina 27360 USA

TABLE OF CONTENTS

Section 1

Introduction..3

Wilderness Journey...5

Being Thrust into a Dry Place...8

Walking through the Wilderness with No End in Sight 12

The Promised Land...18

Preparation Process 22

Promises of God..28

Step One..33

Section 2

An Encounter with Almighty God 37

Stripping to Become First Place.......................................39

Separating to Remain First Place.....................................43

Surrendering—Giving Up to Be Molded 47

Surviving through Prayer and Fasting 51

Settling Who's in Control Once and For All 59

Step Two 63

Section 3

Developing a Relationship: The Secret of Intimacy 67

The Will to Know...68

Drawing Closer: A New Level of Love...76
Step Three...80

Section 4
A Hunger and a Thirst...85
The Heart of God...86
The Head of God...91
Step Four 97

Section 5
The Journey of a Lifetime 101
Learning to Wait on and for God... 102
Moving Levels—Glory to Glory 113
Step Five... 119

Section 6
From the Wilderness to the Promised Land...........................123
Learning Jesus in Life's Journey...125
Being Prepared to Enter Your Promised Land........................132
Step Six 139

Section 7
Conclusion 143
Interventions and Experiences 145
Step Seven 157

SECTION 1

INTRODUCTION

JC and her husband had come from two different worlds; hers a lineage of educators, mainly women, from a prestigious black college in the South. Her parents were kindergarten sweethearts, married over sixty years. Her mother had remained faithful to teaching while her father had served in the army for over twenty-three years, defending the country he loved and making sure his family received benefits from his hard work as he provided for them.

Her husband's family knew a different life, as they were from a coal mining community in Eastern Kentucky. His being the second oldest child and first member of his family to attend college made him quickly stay rooted in God and family.

The two were driven by their love for God, respect for education, commitment to family, and solid core values. The two had vowed to keep the history of their families rooted deep within their heart and home. So they established a little room in their home marked with the treasures of their lineage. JC purposely kept a wooden desk set on bricks in the little room—the priceless gift had been given to her through her lineage. The hundred-year-old desk was engraved with the history of her family's deep roots—dates of birthdays, graduations, marriages, and deaths of loved ones. It even told the history of the voyage of her ancestors from West Africa. All the family lineage was found in this little room called the prayer closet—a room of great sentiment because the most precious item found there was the family Bible that had been passed down from generation to generation, filled with words of loving God, praying, and serving Him above all things. Yet even with so much history stored, JC was about to embark upon a new journey—one unfamiliar to her—a wilderness adventure with no end in sight. .

WILDERNESS JOURNEY

Five years passed before JC would work again in the little room she called her prayer closet. She had converted another space in her home into a study for her husband and herself. But this day, as she passed by the room with a liter of water in her right hand and a small glass and plate in the other, she stopped, placed the water on the floor, and opened the door just in time to see the early morning light breaking through the dingy window that was sealed with a mixture of putty and masking tape. She had never removed the masking tape because she thought it served a good purpose of keeping the wintry air from seeping in during the long cold months.

She picked up the water, walked into the room, and placed it on the floor near the table. She gazed down at the items on the desk—a set of journals, ink pens, a cassette player and several cassette tapes, and the old family Bible. She placed her glass and plate next to a lamp given to her by a friend. .

As she sat down, she found herself thumbing through the pages of one journal marked "Conversations with God." Before she knew it, the sun was setting, and she was reaching for the light switch so she could continue to hover over the materials that brought back memories. As she reached for the string, she realized she didn't have a light bulb. She jumped up from the table, ran to the hallway closet and got a light bulb to place in the lamp. As she continued to read, she found herself sometimes releasing hearty laughter that filled the room. At other times, she found tears streaming down her face. She wept the most as she read words shared by God the Father, who had tenderly walked by her side as she had faced so many trials, heartaches, and challenges.

Late into the night long after JC and her family had finished dinner, she returned to her prayer closet, sat down and , plugged the cassette player into the socket. She held her finger on the play button to listen to the voice that echoed from the cassette player.

Oh, boy! It hasn't taken long this early June morning to realize that my life is in a downward spiral and spinning out of control. I try to place words to the events that are happening as I grab at straws to figure out why I am experiencing such drama. Needless to say, I am still confessing every sin I can think of, even ones I know I have not committed, only to find myself wrestling to hold things together. At this point, I realize I am not in control of anything and feel the need to cry out for help to the One I know as Jesus. I know I have accepted Jesus in my heart, because I believe the words that have come from my mouth professing Him as Lord and Savior. But I can't seem to understand why everything I hold dear and believe is being shaken. All I can ask myself is where is the God I have come to know (or thought I knew), love, and trust? I wonder why God who allows wonderful things to occur in my profession is allowing my private life to become so dysfunctional. I am experiencing conflict and a staleness I have never known. There is major upheaval in my daily routine and I have a negative attitude toward everything including attending church. A feeling of dryness and coldness fills me. I desperately want relief from this desiccation but no matter how much I read my Bible, attend church, or pray, the struggles become greater.

The drama reminds me of a flood or a whirlwind. Each time I fall asleep, my mind drifts back to a couple of dreams where dark clouds travel toward me at great speed. The one dream I cannot shake is where a tornado heads directly for my house and I am hiding in a closet to escape. As I replay the dream, it suddenly becomes evident I am being thrust into a dry place, a place that is new.

BEING THRUST INTO A DRY PLACE

This aridness reminds me of a trip taken by bus to New Mexico. The highway resembles a corridor flanked on both sides by sizzling sand. The bus breaks down, and the radio goes out. It is hot, and there's no air conditioning. The driver cautions impatient passengers about walking away from the bus. As I decide to step to the edge of the sand, I feel the sun beating down upon my face. The desert is a blistering, parched place with dried wood, brush, and sand. It appears to be hotter than the pavement, harboring insects and snakes. It's mostly an uninhabited land that engenders fear as I gaze upon it. It reminds me of two prophets' descriptions of a desert: "a land that lay waste without humans or rain," and "a terrifying land." As my eyes skim over the terrain, I surmise this empty place is a depiction of my existence—hot, dry, bare, and void of life. This dryness plagues my soul and feels like fire burning from the inside out. I cry and plead for this time to be over, but silence fills my heart.

As the cassette tape stopped, the lateness of the hour caught her attention. She stood and glanced around the room. With a , determined look upon her face, she vowed to return later to the little room in order to continue listening to the conversations she'd had with herself, all the while hoping God was listening, too. As she left the room, she pondered over the past events and experiences and the time that had transpired between them. She wondered what would surface from the recorder the next time she played it.

Days later, JC returned to the little room to continue playing the cassette, curious to see what words she had spoken to describe the valley experience. She remembered the encounter had lasted eight months. As she turned the tape over and began to play it, she heard expressions of anguish, doubt, and fear as she described the leaves changing early in September with no relief in sight. Then she heard sniffles and sobs as these words came forth...

> Today, as I enter into my quiet time, there must be an attempt made to find some good in this day; after all, my new job starts today! Even though I feel lifeless and drained from last night's tossing and turning, moving forward is essential to my survival. There must be some message in my daily reading to sustain me this hour. It has been three months, and the days seem like night— the darkness evades my soul. Everything seems to be a crisis and my private life continues to be laced with woes. I am tired of this and want relief. No matter what I read or how I try to manage events, things still are overwhelming and out of control. I cannot continue at this pace. I want a break from the struggles. The more I complain, the worse it seems to get. I still try to find comfort upon the pages of my Bible. I am reading, praying, and doing all I can. What more can I take! I cry, yell, and scream, but God, You don't seem to hear me or want to help me. What else can I do?

JC stopped the tape. So the initial transition was over a three-month period. The negative, despairing approach toward things and her attitude of blaming God for her circumstances alarmed her, and she was determined to stop thinking that way. She surely did not want to relive any of her past, but she also did not want to become so demeaning and harsh toward life, let alone God. She stood and stretched for a few moments, all the while wanting to make sure she sought forgiveness for blaming God. She sat down, turned the tape player on, and heard...

> I must get hold of myself. I can't continue in this state of mind, especially since my new job is an internship to the superintendency. Let me stick with my quiet time routine. Instead of reading from my favorite website, I'll just open the Bible and begin to read. Let's see, Isaiah chapter 43:2-4, What do the words mean? "When you pass through the waters, I will be with you; And through the rivers, they shall not overflow you. When you walk through the fire, you shall not be scorched, nor shall the flame scorch you. For I am the LORD your God, the Holy One of Israel, your Savior; I gave Egypt as your ransom, Ethiopia and Seba in your place. Since you are precious in My sight, since you have been honored and I have love you; therefore, I will give men for you and people for your life." From reading these words, I feel a tingling deep within my soul. Maybe this passage is one to encourage me as I seek to fight the drought within. If I can hang onto these words and believe what I read, maybe things will change. Yes, maybe things will change! Surely this time the Lord is responding to my cry. It has been three months. Maybe this is the breakthrough I need to overcome these challenges I face.

JC paid close attention to the next statements made, because the inflection of her voice changed numerous times just within the opening admission that the dryness continued to linger from October to December. As she sat listening, she knew the set of groans and sighs surfaced because it was it was evident three more months had passed. The only glimpses of life came as the voice on the tape echoed comments such as:

> I am irritated because I find little to no comfort in the daily events and boredom is setting in at a fast pace. I am stuck—I can't move forward! The only thing that holds me together is this internship. I find great comfort in learning new information about my profession. I'm not sure how long I can keep up the façade that all is well. Emotionally, I am drained!

JC paused the tape as her words fell heavily upon her. Could she have been in such despair, under such duress? She pondered over the occurrence that caused her to be a different woman from the one on the tape. Could her answers lie in the journals on the table, on the tape? She reflected over the events and experiences, all the while determined to know the defining moment or moments that can bring a person through challenges. She asked herself, "Is it the same for everyone or are there strategies, ideas, or tidbits one uses to combat challenges? What is the one factor that sparks the change?"

At that point, she prepared to chart the rest of the recordings in hope of finding the tips or tidbits to her survival of a journey that, at the time, had no end in sight.

WALKING THROUGH THE WILDERNESS WITH NO END IN SIGHT

It's late December and I continue to agonize over things and events. I leave church, sit in my car, and listen to Christian radio in an effort to bring relief to my troubled soul. The preaching seems to be good as I hear about a subject called fasting. This preacher talks about corporate fasting and the benefits for one who will fast and seek God. I guess I will research this topic just to learn a little more. I know a little about fasting, but the things this pastor shares seem so electrifying. I think I will try this approach in order to find some solace. What's so surprising, I find it odd that someone has put fasting and seeking God together. I thought I was seeking God as I continue to read and pray. What is the difference to this approach?

The only thing I can do at this time is to find examples of fasting and praying, and to visit this church to see what is really happening. If I attend this church, all I want to do is hear what the preacher says and see if there is material available on the subject. I'll talk to my husband to see if we can visit this Sunday. What can it hurt to visit?

I like the church but with everything else going on, what have I gotten myself into! I know how to keep my mouth closed. I can't believe on a whim I opened my mouth to join in a discussion about serving the Lord. I can't believe I would say to a stranger it has never cost me anything to serve the Lord. What did that lady mean by telling me until it cost me something, I have not experienced the joy of knowing the Lord? I can't believe I am starting a fast at the first of the year with little or no information. All I know is, when I commit to something, it is important to fulfill the commitment. I guess I will see what the twenty-one days bring.

JC sniggered as the tape continued to play. As she stood to take a break, she recalled that since her initial twenty-one-day fast (which had turned into a fast of forty days), she had ventured into many forty-, fifty-, and even a seventy-five-day fast in order to seek the Lord. As she sat back down, she remembered her first fast as though it were yesterday. She focused back on the recording and began to chuckle at herself, thinking how dumb it had been to start something with little to no information and to try a total fast that very first time. She had approached the fast by drinking only bottled water.

The words, "how dumb!" came from the cassette player.

I can't believe I am approaching this fast like this. I know I am a strong-willed woman and I can complete this, but what am I thinking? It is day fourteen, and I keep remembering a hiking trip I took twenty-six years ago. I was away from the comforts of life—sleeping on the ground in a sleeping bag, eating cold food out of a can, and wearing the same clothes without taking a bath. I didn't have a curling iron or makeup. I remember complaining because the real purpose of the trip was to get to know the man I hoped to marry one day, and that wasn't happening. What I thought was important for survival was only a distraction. Because I focused on the wrong things, the trip was hard, long, and boring! Now this fast is like that trip—hard and long! I must remember the purpose of it. It is to seek God and not complain about not having the comforts of life, one of which is food, the very substance—well, the overeating of it—that has caused me to fight a weight problem all these years. Little did I grasp gluttony was a sin! I guess learning new information can be of benefit even if it deals with a tough aspect of one's existence.

Oh well, let me continue to read this book given by the church as a guide to this twenty-one-day fast. As I read each day's reflection along with the Scripture references, I do feel lighter and less emotional over things. I feel cleaner on the inside for some reason. I've been reading my Bible and journaling from a different perspective, too. The pages of the Bible seem to come alive.

JC paused to make a few more notes, and then she continued to listen.

I don't know what the strange presence is as I begin to read today's lesson. There seems to be a sweet presence as I read about Jesus and His forty-day fasting in the wilderness. Did I say, "wilderness"? Hmm…I feel a drawing on the inside to extend my fast from twenty-one days to forty. What is this sweetness lingering over me and this fiery feeling on the inside consuming me but not burning me up?

As I continue in the fast, I want to know more about a wilderness journey. Lord, what is a wilderness journey? Maybe I will get an answer to that question, because the more I read, the more I hear the Lord speaking clearly and succinctly through His Word. In Matthew 4, Jesus' wilderness journey reveals Him as the bread of life who has the protection of His Father. He shows it is important to worship God because He is worthy. *Bingo!* The light bulb is on! For too many years I have just quoted Scripture, but now I understand there is power in God's Holy Word. I need to treat God's Word like food and drink in order to experience the One known as the bread of life. To believe God the Father is important to worshipping the One I love. All I know is His Word says to worship Him. I hear Him saying, "JC, worship Me, for I love you."

What else do I see? Jesus has power to command the enemy to leave Him alone, and that same power is given to any child of God. Jesus was being prepared for a task—that is why He was going through this experience. Matthew 4:17 and 23 state, "From that time Jesus began to preach and to say, 'Repent, for the kingdom of heaven is at hand.… And Jesus went about all Galilee, teaching in their synagogues and preaching the gospel of the kingdom, and healing all kinds of sickness and all kinds of diseases among the people." This Scripture reveals a message from Jesus. He was preaching about the Promised Land, the kingdom of God, and the power of God to heal from the inside out! What do we need to do? *Repent!* Turn from our sins, be healed, and delivered from what plagues the soul.

Lord, at this time I choose not to go through the motions, but I truly want to stop and repent of any sins I have committed. I don't want to just say I have, but I want to ask for Your forgiveness for rebelling against You and Your Word. Hear my heart's cry, please.

There were no words that could describe the feeling that overwhelmed JC as she stopped the machine. She had revisited her past with many different emotions. But at that moment, she felt shame because she remembered how rebellious and controlling she had been, especially with her family. She even remembered how God had placed His finger on areas in her life and she had tried to fix herself without surrendering will to Him. She had allowed her flesh to be her god instead of permitting God the Father, who loved her, to have first place.

She pushed play again, and the words that followed brought a sigh of relief.

It is day forty-two, and newness is emerging. I know change when I feel it. The Word of God comes alive each time I read it like never before. My loving Father is wooing me into a deeper revelation of who He is and an intimate relationship because I have never known an overwhelming love like I know and am experiencing at this time. There is a freshness leading me to see more information about God's love and freedom. What I sense is I am being guided to understand the Lord is the One who liberates people. People cannot set themselves free at all! God shows through His Word, His Son is the God of liberty, and what He wants me to do is present myself to Him through worship and to live totally committed to Him.

I quickly understand the Father has one message as I travel through this wilderness on the path to a deeper walk with Him. I am to follow my Lord by keeping my eyes on Him through this experience so I will reach a promised land He has prepared for me that will bring Him glory.

JC gathered her notes as the tape ended. She carefully stacked her papers and headed to bed, recognizing she had only a couple of hours to sleep before she would have to rise for work. As she laid her head on her pillow, she heard herself thanking the Lord for His persistence. As she closed her eyes, she blew a kiss in the air telling the Father she loved Him. She drifted off to sleep humming, "Jesus loves me, this I know, for the Bible tells me so."

THE PROMISED LAND

JC rose early, preparing to meet the Lord as usual. What had changed since her encounter with the Lord five years earlier was her ability to rise in a worshipful mood. Thirty minutes were spent singing, dancing, praising, and thanking the Lord prior to reading and journaling. Her early mornings were filled with sweetness as she listened for the heart of God. JC had come to enjoy the friendship she had with the Father. As her fellowshipping with the Lord concluded that morning, she readied herself for work. JC was determined to listen to the tape on her hour commute to her worksite, so she stopped by the little room and grabbed the cassette player and her notes. She packed them in her book bag and ran out to her car. As she made her way to the expressway and merged onto the highway, she pushed play and heard laughter. This was different from the past. Previously, she'd heard sighs, groans, and crying, but this morning she heard laughter. Following the laughter came the words:

> To learn about a promised land, I guess I will reread the book of Exodus. There is so much I have never seen before. Even though my fast is complete, I find myself in a partial fast because I want the revelation of God's Word to remain fresh and alive. Today, as I study the various aspects of the book of Exodus, I'll ask God to

step off the pages of His Word and bring greater insight to it. As I read, what do I see about God? I see how He:

- revealed Himself (I AM) to Moses and then to the people in such unique ways;
- described the land before the Israelites had ever set out on their journey;
- taught (commanded) them to worship and celebrate who He was;
- shared promises as they became and remained obedient; and
- revealed Himself as El Shaddai, God Almighty, (Exodus 6:3) through the tabernacle (Exodus 25–27).

What else do I see? Let me read and review these references listed. Hmm…I am reading about a people in bondage to Egypt, a powerful nation, for over four hundred years. What type of bondage and what does Egypt represent? The bondage appears to have been spiritual as well as physical. The spiritual bondage was their inability to worship the God who had introduced Himself to:

- Abraham as El Elyon, the Most High God, maker of heaven and earth (Genesis 14:19–20), El Shaddai, I am God almighty (Genesis 17:1) and Jehovah Jireh, the Lord will provide (Genesis 22:14);
- Isaac as a sanctuary, shelter, safe haven, or dwelling place (Genesis 26); and
- Jacob as El Elohe-Israel, the God of Israel (Genesis 33:20).

Basically, they were not able to worship El Berith, the God of the covenant (Genesis 13:14–17, 15:18–21 and 17:1–8), whose promise and provision are everything. God's signature upon the Hebrew people is the revelation of who He is as He reveals in His Word. As I read I see a pattern. First of all, a group of people experienced a wilderness journey with a promise of entering into a land prepared for them and then Jesus experiences a wilderness encounter, followed by His preaching of a promised land.

The Hebrews' physical bondage was a forced labor, harsh and brutal. Through whippings and excessive hours of work, the Hebrew people built Egypt. To the natural eye, Egypt represented all that was good—world power, prominence, wealth, and freedom. But to the spiritual eye, Egypt seems to have been a symbol of the world (the flesh; sinful nature) with all its idols and gods enticing mankind into a false worship.

As I dig deeper, I read how God took one person, Moses, from among the Hebrews, saved him as an infant, allowed him to rise in the world and brought him from the world's mountaintop to God's valley of decision. Moses decided who he was and his purpose as God stripped and rebuilt him for His work. Moses had to experience the back side of life in order to move into the place where God could use him for His greater glory. God moved Moses from Egypt (the world), to and through the desert (his wilderness encounter), to Midian (a holding place), and then back to Egypt as a new man shaped for the service of God. Moses had to walk the path with no one other than God and be prepared to learn of the One who introduced Himself as I AM.

A closer look reveals that Moses had two wilderness experiences. Both times he left Egypt. The first experience took forty years as God removed the world from him in order to prepare him for service. The second time Moses left Egypt never to return. He left with a vision, a mission, the wealth of Egypt, and a desire to fulfill his calling or his ministry unto the Father, coupled with his commission to lead God's people to the Promised Land.

The second wilderness experience revealed a very humble man (Numbers 12:3). He shared an intimate walk with the Father. As Moses drew closer to God, he sat face-to-face with God (Exodus 33:11). As God refined the relationship, Moses walked through this process and communed with God for the souls of the people (intercessory prayer) and the work of the kingdom.

God revealed Himself through nature and demonstrated His power through signs and wonders. He showed Himself as a blazing fire in the midst of a bush (Exodus 3:2), and a cloud by day and a pillar of fire by night (Exodus 13:21). He demonstrated His power through ten plagues and parting the Red Sea. He revealed His presence among His chosen through thunder, lightning, and a thick cloud upon His Mountain. He provided manna, the bread of life, throughout their journey as the source of life.

The land given was the land of the Canaanites, Hittites, Amorites, Perizzites, Hivites and the Jebusites. Exodus chapter 3 gives a description of the land that God provided—a good and spacious land flowing with milk (strength, full of nutrients) and honey (natural sweetness, beauty). It was a land of great substance (wheat and barley, vines, fig trees, pomegranates, olive oil, brooks of water, fountains, and springs flowing forth in valleys and hills, Deuteronomy 8:7–8) that yielded a harvest second to none. The land was for His chosen, the ones on whom He bestowed favor for a lifetime because of who He is, El Berith, the God of the covenant. God also gave them the wealth of Egypt (Exodus 3:21–22). I believe He gave it to them to repay them for their years of work in Egypt as He prepared and taught them how to give to Him and prospered them so they would enter the Promised Land a wealthy people, lacking nothing.

PREPARATION PROCESS

JC continued listening to the tape as she drove to work

> Preparation process, what is that? I see where God taught them to worship and celebrate who He is by giving them seven feasts, the first of which was the Passover (Exodus 12:12–51). The Father showed His love by *acknowledging* the power of the blood as He said, "Now the blood shall be a sign for you on the houses where you are. And when I see the blood, I will pass over you; and the plague shall not be on you to destroy you when I strike the land of Egypt." (Exodus 12:13). Thus He *demonstrated* His authority over Egypt while saving the firstborn sons of Israel.
>
> I notice God taught Israel the significance of sanctifying unto Him every firstborn, the first offspring of every womb among the sons of Israel, both of man and beast. He revealed the importance of devoting to Him what He deemed of value to Him—Jesus, His Son, who was sanctified unto Him as the firstborn male of all creation. Jesus devoted Himself to the Father and His mission while on earth, becoming the sacrifice for man's transgressions.

JC turned into the parking lot at the central office. As she parked the car, these words came through the tape:

> What is so important about God teaching people how to do things? What other things did God teach them?

> I am tired and must continue at a later date. At least my emotions seem under control, even though my husband fell off a ladder and tore his rotator cuff and the boys still struggle with the college lifestyle. I believe they will return to the Lord and get off the track of enjoying the world.

JC remained in the car long enough to rewind the tape to hear those last statements. She was curious as to what she had meant about God teaching people things, and she wanted to hear the tone and message about her emotions being under control. She reached for paper and pencil and made a quick note as she listened again to the final remarks on the tape. At the end of her comments, she bundled up, grabbed her book bag, and made her way to her office.

JC was taught early in life to treat people the way she wanted to be treated; therefore, she greeted everyone with a smile. This was also the stance of this district as shared by her mentor. He made it a point to remind her that the position of superintendent was one of great influence and one day when she became a superintendent, it would be important for the people to see their leader modeling courtesy, respect, and a genuine regard for all people. It wasn't hard for JC to display those characteristics because she believed a smile and kind words had an impact on a person's day.

JC opened her door, hung up her coat, and put her book bag beside her computer. She logged on and took a few minutes to review her emails. As she began to review her calendar for the day, she realized she would have a light workload. She was assigned to visit schools that day and afterward would be able to leave early. Normally, her days didn't end before 6:00 p.m., because her mentor had so many meetings to attend.

When her phone rang, to her surprise, her mentor informed her that he would be working out of the district that day and wanted her to attend a meeting near her home at ten o'clock. His further instructions sparked her heart. He told her not to return to the office because it would be senseless to leave the meeting and drive an hour back to the office only to have to turn around and head back home. Instead, she was told to go home after the meeting and start preparing a briefing for a meeting that would occur within the next three days. What great news! She began to organize the things needed for the meeting and shared with the secretary her change in schedule. She stopped at the receptionist's desk, picked up the directions to the meeting, and made her way to her car. It seemed as though her prayers were answered. She could listen to the other side of the tape on her way to the meeting to learn more answers to her questions. She set the tape, pushed play, and as she backed out, began to listen again.

How did God teach the Israelitest to worship and celebrate? God brings and reveals. In the Bible, it says God brought them to His mountain (a face-to-face encounter). It looked like God was doing what I call a show-and-tell in order to teach, develop, and build their faith in Him and lavish them with His love. He taught them how to know His voice and obey His commands. He revealed their ultimate purpose by declaring all the sons of Israel (men, women, and children) were His, a kingdom of priests and a nation holy to Him (Exodus 19:5–6). And if they were all priests, they would perform their priestly duties, namely worshipping God in spirit and truth. Through His face-to-face encounter, He showed that worship and celebrating go hand in hand, and He receives that worship when people sanctify and devote themselves to Him. Basically, pure worship before God is the presentation of the whole self—heart, mind, body, and soul—as a living and holy sacrifice before Him. The Hebrews were to come before Him with steadfast a spirit, a broken, and contrite heart, which God will not despise (Psalm 51:10, 17). They were to make a joyful shout to the Lord and serve Him with gladness, to enter into His gates with thanksgiving and His courts with praise (Psalm 100:1–2, 4), and to sing, dance, and play their instruments before Him (Exodus 15) as a sacrifice unto the Father.

As she made her way through town to get to the expressway, JC pulled in at a gas station to fill up, but mainly to jot down a few more notes. The information generated a need in her to reread her Bible when she arrived home. After she filled her gas tank, she headed to the highway with her heart racing with excitement over what might be heard next and she listened intently.

How do I know God revealed Himself to them? What is found on the pages of the Bible that will provide me with the answer? Okay, it says God spoke to Moses to let him know He was appearing to the Hebrews in a new way, another level of His love as the Father, Son, and Holy Spirit. I see words God is speaking.

He says, "I appeared to Abraham, Isaac and Jacob, as God Almighty [El Shaddai], but by My name, Lord, I was not known to them" (Exodus 6:3). But he told Moses to say to the sons of Israel, "I am the Lord" (Exodus 6:6) and "I have remembered my covenant" (Exodus 6:5), and "I will give it to you as a heritage; I am the Lord" (Exodus 6:8). Okay, so God wanted them to worship and celebrate who He is as He lavished His love on them. Based on meeting God through a mountaintop experience, the children of Israel were to sanctify themselves.

What is this I am reading now? Exodus 19:16 says that there were thunderings and lightnings and a thick cloud on the mountain, and the sound of the trumpet was very loud. All the people in the camp trembled. This was an unbelievable yet awesome encounter! I am amazed at what I see next. Let me read this aloud. "Moses brought the people out of the camp to meet with God, and they stood at the foot of the mountain" (Exodus 19:17). "Then Moses went up with Aaron, Nadab and Abihu, and seventy of the elders of Israel, and they saw the God of Israel; and there was under His feet as it were a paved work of sapphire stone, and it was like the very heavens in its clarity. But on the nobles of the children of Israel He did not lay His hand. So they saw God and they ate and drank" (Exodus 24:9–11).

As I read further, the description of the text is so awe-inspiring. Look at the position of the people! They were at the base of the holy mountain of God where they could worship at the feet of God. He allowed them the opportunity to gain clarity that if they are going to serve Him and obey His commandments, position was important because it was the entry level to Him. I get it. Coming as a lowly subject to the Almighty and reverencing (praising and worshipping) Him as holy is where the heart of God meets and claims the heart of man. It was at that point God reminded them of His covenant, His sealed agreement, with Abraham that was ratified through blood. Exodus 24:8 states that "And Moses took the blood, sprinkled it on the people, and said, 'This is the blood of the covenant, which the Lord has made with you according to all these words.' " What words? God gave them His words of love—His Ten Commandments, the laws, rights, and responsibilities (Exodus 20–23)—and sealed them through His covenant. In the sealed agreement of love are the promises of God!

PROMISES OF GOD

The meeting was held in the regional office of with school districts across the state.. JC made sure she had her private notes and the notebook from her district. She slid her private notes into the district's folder in case she had a few minutes before the meeting to glance over what she had written. As she entered the building, the receptionist directed her to the meeting room where she was informed that several superintendents would be late, so she could get lunch and come back or just wait. JC's eyes lit up with exhilaration at what she would do with her time. She would review her notes and go over all that she had been hearing over the last couple of days. As she sat down and sunlight peeped through the curtains, she remembered the first time she walked into her little room as the sunrise broke through the faded window. Now she asked herself, What has God promised? Just as she thought about the question, the superintendents began to enter the room.

The meeting was long but insightful. She knew she had to take good notes because her mentor was such a detail-oriented man that he would want to know every comment made and all items discussed. As the meeting adjourned, she smiled, wished everyone a good day, and then made a dash to the door and to the parking lot. She settled herself in the car and prepared for the thirty-minute drive home. To keep from wasting time, she decided to grab dinner for her husband so she could have more time to listen and review her tapes. At home, she found a note from her husband about trying to reach her by cell phone. He would be late that night because of a meeting. What perfect timing! After resting for a few moments, JC decided to continue listening.

She pushed play as she grabbed her paper and pen.

What promises does God make? Moses tells the people that the Lord their God would test them. Even in the midst of their griping and whining, God provided focus for them on their journey by stating, "If you diligently heed the voice of the Lord your God and do what is right in His sight, give ear to His commandments and keep all His statutes, I will put none of the diseases on you which I have brought on the Egyptians; for I am the Lord who heals you." (Jehovah Rohe) (Exodus 15:26). He then provided water and palm trees (Jehovah Jireh) (Exodus 15:27), rained bread from heaven which they called manna (Exodus 16:4), and waged war against Amalek from generation to generation (Jehovah Nissi, The Lord is my Banner) (Exodus 17:15–16).

> What revelation! I am seeing names for God I have not known, as well as other feasts. The Father continued to share His promises with the people as He guided them through the wilderness. God established three national feasts to be celebrations to Him. The promises attached to the three national feasts—the Feast of Unleavened Bread, the Feast of the Harvest of the First Fruits, and the Feast of the Ingathering—were sevenfold (Exodus 23):
>
> - v. 20—sending An angel before them to keep them in the way and to bring them into the place which God had prepared;
> - v. 22—being an enemy to their enemies and an adversary to their adversaries;
> - v. 25—blessing their bread and water;

- v. 25—taking sickness from their midst;
- v. 26—protecting the womb so that no one would miscarry or be barren in their land; fulfilling the number of their days;
- v.—causing confusion among all the people to whom they come and will make all their enemies turn their backs on them
- v. 30—driving out the inhabitants of the Promised Land little by little so they would be ready to take possession of the land.

Then God shared what He would do if they walked in His statutes and kept His commandments (Leviticus 26). He would:

- v. 4—give them rains in their season so that the land would yield its produce and the trees of the field would bear their fruit;
- v. 5—cause their threshing to last till the time of vintage, and their vintage shall last till the time of sowing;
- v. 5—eat their bread to the full and dwell in the land safely;
- v. 6—give peace in the land so they shall lie down and none will make them afraid;
- v. 6—rid the land of evil beasts, and the sword will not go through the land;
- v. 7—chase their enemies and put them to flight—five shall chase a hundred and a hundred shall chase ten thousand;
- v. 8—their enemies shall fall by the sword before them

- v. 9—look on them favorably and make them fruitful and multiply them; confirm the covenant with them;
- v. 11—set His tabernacle among them and His soul shall not abhor them; and
- v. 12—walk among them and be their God and they shall be His people.

All these promises were given from a loving Father to His children. God showed His unconditional love for His children when He declared, "I drew them with gentle cords, with bands of love" (Hosea 11:4), yet His promises were conditioned upon their obedience in keeping His commandments and statutes. The Scriptures state the Lord keeps His words. They are "pure words; as silver tried in a furnace of earth, purified seven times" (Psalm 12:6–7). He chose to keep His promises to them by remaining as the cloud by day and pillar of fire by night, but even greater than that, He allowed them to build Him a dwelling place, His sanctuary; His tabernacle among them.

JC put her pen on top of her notes and sat back to reflect what she had learned. She had an intense desire to collect her thoughts based on her experience and what she had received from reading her Bible through a different set of lenses. She understood a wilderness journey was about one's spiritual growth so when one entered his promised land, he would be able to reap the benefits God had prepared for him. JC had come to value prayer, fasting, and worshipping because they were great spiritual disciplines that brought a person in line with God's Word and His purpose. The overarching lesson gained through her wilderness journey was the discovery God the Father desired communion with people and He had gone to great lengths to save their souls, having sent His Son to save mankind so none would perish! Next to God's love for His Son is His love for people!

She glanced down at the last note she had written. "The dryness faded as I continued to read daily of His love. On the pages of His Word, I could hear Him say, "JC, tell people I love them, adore them, and care deeply for them. Tell them to come to Me, their tabernacle, their sanctuary—for My Son stands ready to receive them and present them to Me!"

Step One

Stop Being a Pessimist! Become an Optimist!

John 16:33 states, "In the world you will have tribulation. But be of good courage! I have overcome the world." We are also told to "Count it all joy, my brothers and sisters, when you fall into various trials knowing that the testing of your faith produces patience." (James 1:2–3). So the key learning is to recognize adversity and respond to it in a manner pleasing unto the Lord. Just remember: Adversity is a tool used to build faith.

Take a few minutes to reflect over this section to stimulate your thinking.

Word Study: pessimist, optimist, wilderness, worship, fasting

1. A _____ is a person who has a tendency to focus on the negative or to take the gloomiest possible view. An _____ is a person who has the tendency to focus on the positive even when things are not going well.
2. A _____ journey is a spiritual voyage taken to enhance one's growth.
3. _____ is a spiritual discipline where one willingly abstains from food or drink for a period of time.

4. _____ is the act of praising, giving honor, and devoting oneself to God.

Questions:

1. What challenges or trials are you facing? Why do you think you are facing them?
2. Describe your attitude towards everything. Are you negative, positive, or unsure?
3. What are your dreams, hopes, or aspirations? Are they in line with God's will for you?

Tips:

1. Get a journal and begin to write about what is occurring in your life.
2. Research fasting. Pray and decide what God would have you to do.
3. Begin to worship God. Spend time reading and praying God's Word instead of focusing on your problems.

SECTION 2

AN ENCOUNTER WITH
ALMIGHTY GOD

JC's fellowship with the Lord truly had taken on a new and fresh meaning. She was eager to meet with Him to learn more of what His Word said. Before she listened to another tape, she decided to thumb through one of the journals stacked on the table. As she thumbed through she grabbed one journal with the heading marked "An Encounter with Almighty God—a promise made!" JC was curious about the last part of the heading marked "a promise made" so she looked to see if there was a sticky note with a clue, but there wasn't a hint of anything. She pondered over the statement. Then she asked herself had she made a promise to God during this journey, and if so, what was it?

JC paused, giggled a little as she put her hand on her forehead, and shook her head as she stated she had remembered completing a survey at a church retreat. The survey was based on a scale of one to ten. You were asked to share where God fit into your life. She remembered reading her list where she had place God somewhere on that list, but where. She listened to find out what transpired during this season of life as well as what promise had been made.

In all that I have experienced over these months, the one thing that God continues to remind me of is His desire to be first place. It is the hardest thing to give up control and trust someone I have never seen. This has been the struggle since college—matter of fact, all my life.

JC talked right along with the tape as it continued to play. She wanted to know where did God fit in her walk, and if anything had He moved to number one. She pondered over a promise made-had she promised God she would stop trying to control things or what? As she continued to listen, she knew things had changed because of the encounter she had with God.

STRIPPING TO BECOME FIRST PLACE

The memory years gone by was sketchy to say the least, but one thing she knew was God had continuously placed people in her path to share the importance of Him being first place. There was fear that caused stubbornness to surface. It prevented her from trusting and allowing God to have control. If anyone was to ask her now, she would provide a different answer to trusting God. As she thought about the situation, she believed God had a more relevant role and position. . She knew she had experienced God and was sure He was an integral part even to the point of Him being first place.

As JC headed to bed, she chuckled at the thought that crossed her mind—the thought focused on how, five years ago, she had basically determined what, when, and where she wanted God to intervene. She recalled how, when things seemed out of control by her standards, she would turn to a more intense reading and praying routine, and then when things appeared to calm down, she would slip back into control mode again, thanking God while at the same time letting Him know she could and would assume control once again. As she laid her head on her pillow, she pondered over the mere fact she could not remember making a promise to God. Her closing prayer was a plea for help—a cry for Him to bring to memory the promise she had made to Him.

Morning seem to come much sooner. JC woke unusually early and moved into a time of worship. With her question lingering in her mind, she decided to read her journal first before listening to her tape. As she opened her journal and read several pages, she began to see phrases like "stripping," "God's power to strip one's life" and "He stripped me of self." Her statement about a promise made to God faded as she felt a powerful tug on her heart to find out more about the action that caused her to write, "He stripped me of self."

JC turned on the cassette player to the words that sent her mind racing. She began to clearly remember the events that sent her life into a downward spiral.

> I have become more and more a part of the world—a world where materialism and pleasure, ambition and drive, and work beyond the duty-day have become king. I have left my first love, and I don't even know how far I have drifted from the initial love affair where I knelt at the foot of the cross. To top things off, I am experiencing major upheaval daily. Major setbacks have occurred and medical bills have increased due to the fact my husband and I both have had unexpected surgeries. Every time I turn around there appears to be one catastrophe after another. Lord, please tell me what is going on!

JC touched the stop button and as she continued to turn the pages of the journal, she began to see words she knew she would not have said herself. She read, "JC, your enemy has done this to you." As JC continued to read, faded ink spots were visible where she'd cried at the message she had received from the Father. Her next sentences confirmed her innermost fears. She had written,

Little did I realize over the years, I had b not surrendered much of my time and relationship to God. I see how the world has taken first place. The Lord is showing me through my readings and conversations with Him that I have been a prisoner of generational curses and I have allowed the world to rule by permitting rebellion, unbelief, impatience, self-centeredness, control, lust, greed, and pride to become kings. I have fallen into the trap of the enemy and self.

As JC turned on the tape player, she listened intently as her voice trembled at describing what God declared in His word for her. She heard herself reading Scripture, "Is this not the fast I have chosen: to loose the bonds of wickedness, to undo the heavy burdens, to let the oppressed go free and that you break every yoke?" (Isaiah 58:6) This verse was followed by: "The things which are impossible with men are possible with God" (Luke 18:27). JC continued to listen to a description of events that built upon each other and began a process of freedom for her.

The next series of statements revealed the change that had set her on the path to reestablish her relationship with God. She described how she knew God had placed His finger on her to fast. She also described how she encountered God at two women's retreats in ways she had never before experienced. She listened as she described how God began to burn pride (that has many faces) out of her during the first women's retreat simply by letting her know He was "a consuming fire" (Hebrews 12:29). God reminded her that He, "the Lord, whose name is Jealous, is a jealous God" (Exodus 34:14). She described the details of the second retreat, recounting that God had declared He was stripping her of self and the world and when He built her back up, she would know a love full of fire, a blazing fire He had always wanted her to know and experience. JC recorded how as the speaker began to share, it had seemed as though God had taken a knife and started to perform an intense surgical procedure inside of her. JC began to cry bittersweet tears as she remembered how rejection had plagued her soul, but she had finally heard a message of love—the message God had been trying to share with her for so many years. For some unknown reason, she had not learned how to receive the love of God.

JC was not prepared for the next thing she encountered. As she listened, she heard how God had not only stripped the inside of her but the outside as well. He began stripping her of the pleasures of the world. In the comments following, she was reminded God had declared she would not be put to shame, neither was she to feel humiliated, for she would not be disgraced because He was the God of all the earth. The last words on the tape were ones JC had rehearsed over and over in her mind—the words she felt God had impressed upon her heart. Those words were, "I am trying to give you My best, JC, for 'I know the thoughts that I think toward you,…thoughts for peace and not of evil to give you a future and a hope" (Jeremiah 29:11).

As the tape ended, JC flipped open her journal to the last page that coincided with the tape. She found a section highlighted in bright yellow and circled in orange. The section began, "I will serve the Lord all the days of my life!" Then she read, "JC, that is what you told Me." JC sensed God had reminded her of the vow she had made so many years ago, and He was ready for her to fulfill her vow unto Him at His level of commitment and timing. Her closing words were, "I guess for God to get what He wants—intimacy and first place in my life—He had to strip me of self."

JC moved from her table and went about her day completing tasks. She thought about the stripping process and began to think about the next step in God's process of dealing with His children.

Separating to Remain First Place

The day went well at work for JC. She completed tasks and made it a point to write any thought that came to mind that might give her a clue as to the strategies one uses to define the stages of growth. She knew she had ventured through a major change to get to where she was in her walk with the Lord. At the end of her workday, she decided to carve out a couple of hours in order to scan through her journals to find the next series of messages she had recorded and written about her encounter with God.

As she made her way to her prayer room, she pulled out what she had written throughout the day about strategies in a growth process. She placed her paper on the table, hoping to find words that might support her thinking. As she glanced through the thickness of the journal, there were blue sticky notes used as markers, scribbled with words like *separating, surrendering, surviving,* and *settling.* The first marker was entitled "Separating to Remain First Place." She read that section, finding where she had defined the word *separate,* followed by a note to listen to the tape labeled "Being Separated by God for His Work." JC found the tape, placed it in the cassette player, and heard herself say,

> *Separate* means to be pulled apart from something. God, my Father, here is what I see You doing as read Your

word. You must tear things off me in order to establish Your presence and reveal Your call. I am experiencing this separation as You build a lasting relationship with me. Lord, I sense You saying that, unless people are willing to be separated to answer the call upon their lives, they cannot truly serve You as You so desire. Unless they separate, they will never know what is real and what is not! Lord, continue to separate me for Your work so I may know what is real!

"*Wow!*" Several memories surfaced as JC ceased the tape. She returned to her journal and as she read, her entry it was the first portion of the encounter followed by the statement from the tape.

This separation thing is something to contend with for I am not one who wants to be separated from people... but again, God is showing me who's in charge. I cannot believe God is showing me how this separation process is to work. All I know is, as I prayed over an unfortunate choice my oldest child made, I felt a strong and powerful pull in my spirit to release him into God's hands. Dumb, dumb me, I chose to try to pull back, to hang on to him. The more I pulled, the stronger the grip was on the other end. As soon as I released him, I felt the Lord lining up my second child. I started tugging to hang on to him, but the powerful jerk from the other end was so overwhelming, I had to release him, too. With the boys out of my grasp, I just gave the Lord my husband. What You have done, Lord, is break them free of my controlling behavior and set a barrier between them and me long enough for You to have

control and strip me of self. Lord, I sense You telling me
to fast for ten days so You will have my full attention.
What is it You want?

JC's finger was in the normal position to push play. She was hoping
to hear words that would give more detail to the separating process.
She was right! The information from the tape gave more insight to
what God wanted from her. She listened as she heard herself describing
how God had put His finger on two television programs that seemed
funny and harmless, and how she had come to understand they were
shows that glorified the world's behavior. She noticed how she stated
she would not watch the pictures ever again, even the reruns, because
they were directly advocating immoral behavior. JC noticed the next
statements focused on how she had not contacted her children or close
friends the days while she fasted. She was giving God her full attention
and watching for any signs He wanted her to change something else in
her behavior. As she continued to listen, references were references made
to God separating or setting people apart—including a nation—so His
purpose would be fulfilled. She even stated she understood what God
wanted from her. But her next comments alluded to the fact she hadn't
quite gotten the learning like she thought.

> Boy! God is something else! I cannot believe I have
> put my foot in my mouth by saying I need someone
> to talk to, and God is responding to that statement by
> asking me is He enough for me? All I can say is I hear
> You, Lord, and You are enough for me. I will remember
> You are the Lord who has separated me unto You and
> sanctified me. I know no one can separate me from Your
> love. I acknowledge You are the person I am to talk to
> each and every day. You want nothing between us but

love and devotion. I am learning You are enough for me as You continue to separate me for Your pleasure.

At the end of the tape, JC reminded herself to write three phrases in her journal as a constant focus of her new learning. Those reminders were:

- everyone who is called by His name is separated unto Him for His purpose,
- the separation is critical in order to be able to hear, see, and experience God's presence as one comes to know His will, and
- loving God and being devoted unto Him is His heart's desire for each person.

SURRENDERING—GIVING
UP TO BE MOLDED

The second sticky note had the word *surrender* written in big capital letters. JC laughed because she sensed the drama conveyed through those letters. As she turned the next page, she saw, "I must learn the words to the song, 'I Surrender All.' " It was at this point, boldness had developed in her relationship with God. This time as she played the tape, the same words on the tape appeared in her journal. She had written the words down verbatim so she would remember this conversation with God.

> Now, God, I grew up hearing the song, "I Surrender All," and I know I have surrendered my all to You. I have watched You strip and separate me; therefore, I have surrendered to You. Don't You understand, I have done all You have asked of me. I have given You my soul for all eternity. I have given You my family and my job, so what's left for You to have? I hear You telling me to trust and obey You, and I do. Along with the trust and obey, You have reminded me of Your Son and His death upon the cross, so what else do You want from me? Say what? Give my life to You? What else is there to give You? Surrender my life to You?

As the tape continued to play, no words surfaced. JC fast-forwarded the tape while flipping over to the third sticky note. There she read of her resistance to this new command from God. She expressed great fear of giving her life to the Father as she tried to rationalize her thoughts of commitment. She read many words that seemed to say she had surrendered, but none of them appeared genuine. JC pushed play. Then she heard a few words about a face-to-face encounter, so she rewound the tape to find the beginning of the message of someone having a face-to-face meeting, all the while knowing she was the one who had a face-to-face encounter with God. As the tape began, she gasped for breath as she remembered the night she had the most precious vision of Christ. She played this message over and over until the warmth she felt that night lingered upon her. She paid close attention to every word.

The process of surrendering to God has begun. As I attempt to stay away from the Father because I fear the command to surrender, emptiness surfaces in my soul. The only way to change the feeling is to move forward; therefore, I will attend the all-night prayer session to work on this feeling.

JC continued to listen with intensity. The description of the first prayer session sparked her heart.

Well, as usual, God let me know He was in charge. As I sat in the session, the most profound experience occurred. The minister opened with praise and worship, followed by prayer at the altar. As I returned to my seat, an outline was given as a guide to the lesson that would be presented. Little was I prepared for the lesson on a place called "Peniel." The minister had us read from Genesis 32:28–30 with a focus on verse 30. I asked myself what was a Peniel experience? The answer followed as the minister taught about Jacob having a face-to-face encounter with God and his life was preserved. At the close of the teaching, the minister directed all of us to close our eyes and pray for God to meet us face-to-face as we surrendered to Him.

I began to pray, but before I could get the words out of my mouth, I saw Jesus in a vision walking up a hill with a cross on His back. I was jumping around and talking to Him. He looked at me as He carried His cross. He was beaten and bruised. I could see His face. He never said a word, but I continued to talk to Him. The next thing I saw was Him hanging on the cross and me at the foot of it. Instantly He was transformed wearing a white robe with His arms outstretched. He had a smile on His face, and I knew He was bidding me to come to Him. At that moment, I found myself stepping face forward into His arms. As I turned around, my back was against His chest. His arms, which were enclosed in His white robe, covered me securely. I sat up immediately after I saw His arms wrap around me and a smile on His face. I opened my journal, listening for God—but I began to write the words, "I surrender to You this hour—I really do surrender to You!"

JC stopped everything and began to worship the Father as she sang, "I Surrender All." It was evident three things had began to emerge that were valuable. They were:

- listening more and talking less as God taught her about His love;
- finding true freedom in her Savior as she surrendered her life; and
- experiencing intimacy daily with the Father was vital.

SURVIVING THROUGH PRAYER AND FASTING

The same journal, marking an encounter with God seemed to hold a special meaning as JC refreshed herself over the section that was thick and had plenty of details about prayer and fasting. JC had known her prayer life had changed and she did contribute it to the time she spent studying how people in the Bible prayed and fasted. She even remembered reading how Jesus prayed often, even sometimes praying all night long. JC believed she had only scratched the surface in this area but had stated she was committed to learning more because of the transformation that had occurred in her.

In her early years, many questions had risen as to why one should pray and fast. Because of the question, JC studied everything she could find about the way Jesus prayed. She also studied how others in the Bible prayed. She read books written by preachers on prayer and fasting. It seemed she wanted to find the main reason why one should pray. She realized she had been moved from praying prayers of "thank you for keeping a roof over our head and blessing us with jobs" to reverencing Him for who He was and wanting to know the heart of the Father. A quick glance at a pile of tapes stacked on top of each other led JC to understand the stack was all marked as being on prayer and fasting. In her journal, she had written she was learning to pray like Jesus did in John 17. JC was filled with great anticipation to be reminded about what had transpired in this particular season of hers.

> Lord, why does one pray? What is the importance of prayer? What's the importance of fasting? I know I fast because You have declared I should, but why? Okay, I plan to study so I may know the answers to these questions. It's as though these questions hold the key and I really want to grow. Let's see, as I do this word search, I find there are over 191 references to prayer or praying coupled with examining the position of those mentioned. It seems no matter the physical position—the heart, mind, and soul have to be in one accord before the Father. Prayer is communicating with the Father and listening for His voice. It is important to establish a relationship and remember prayer is the vital source, the lifeline to God. So I need to learn what happens when I pray and how to recognize those answers. The one point that continues to surface in my study is the way Jesus prayed for people. Jesus' focus is on more spiritual matters than physical things. I see Jesus' prayers being directed to salvation, wholeness, love, and so many other things. Now this is strange. Christ is praying for me while He is in heaven. This is way too much for me to handle. Let me slow down and see if I get this—Christ is my Intercessor and has left examples of how He prayed for people (His disciples), and how He expects us to pray for people. So, I now understand we are to be intercessors as Christ is by

constantly praying for others as well as for their needs and all spiritual matters.

The more I study prayer, the more I see fasting connected as an important factor to spiritual freedom and restoration. Prayer combined with fasting was a lifestyle for Jesus. He demonstrated the importance of winning spiritual battles and breaking strongholds. As I read the Bible, I find winning souls—the salvation of souls—is a top priority; of utmost importance because Jesus will be returning soon. He needs warriors doing battle for the souls of mankind, and He needs them now! I have learned fasting is abstaining from an activity such as eating or sleeping, but always committing the activity as unto the Lord.

Isaiah 58 was mentioned in church as the fasting chapter of the Bible. It is important for me to read this chapter to learn the essence of fasting. As I read verse 5, it reveals fasting as "a day for man to afflict his soul, bowing one's head like a bulrush and for spreading out sackcloth and ashes." What I see is fasting is basically a period of time to humble oneself with penitence before God. Isaiah 58:6 tells of what God declares He will do for a person who fasts unto Him. It is important to remember God will loose or undo the attachment or relationship of anything that is a dominion, load, weight, or bondage as it plagues my soul. He will smash, destroy, shatter, crush, or pound everything that grasps, seizes, embraces, sticks, or clutches me as a prisoner. So when I yield myself to God through fasting and praying, my temple is purged of bondages that seek to control and keep me from living a holy life acceptable unto God. clarity

As JC skimmed through her notes, she found information pertaining to both individual and national fasts. She had highlighted words that seemed to bring clarity to the importance of fasting and praying. In a very upbeat voice, she read.

In Matthew 4:2, the Scriptures reveal Jesus fasted forty days and forty nights in preparation for His ministry. He received power from on high to do the work God had sent Him to do. He fasted during His time on earth. He humbled His soul through fasting and prayer to teach people the significance of seeking God and to be sensitive to spiritual things.

JC reread her journal entries because the focus on fasting and prayer emerged from the Father's conversation about the reason for fasting and what He wanted to do with His people in order to bring souls to Him. As JC reviewed the list of names, she looked closely at the reason for the fast and the outcome of the fast. The names were:

- Moses fasted before the Lord for forty days without eating and drinking, in order to receive direction and guidance as He led the Israelites. He gained more than he would ever know—the Lord gave the Law; the Ten Commandments for all mankind (Exodus 34:27–28).
- Elijah fasted for forty days and nights for guidance and direction. He received revelation that Elisha would be the prophet in his place and that there were seven thousand in Israel who had not bent their knee to Baal (1 Kings 19:8, 16, 18).

- Samuel fasted at least one day, repenting for the false worship that had taken place among the Israelites (1 Samuel 7:6).

- David lay prostrate before the Lord all night on the ground interceding for the life of the child born out of his adulterous affair with Bathsheba. He was seeking mercy from God which ultimately restored David's relationship with God (2 Samuel 12:16).

- Nehemiah fasted for days on behalf of Israel because they had not kept the commandments, statues, or ordinances of God. God delivered him from his enemies and gave him instruction on ratifying and restoring the Covenant of God (Nehemiah 1:4).

- Daniel fasted for ten days to avoid defiling himself before God (Daniel 1:12) and twenty-one days to gain understanding of the vision God had given (Daniel 10:2–3).

- Anna fasted night and day in the temple. Fasting and praying were her lifestyle. God allowed her to testify to the presence of Christ Jesus when Mary and Joseph brought the baby Jesus to the temple to fulfill the requirements of the Law (Luke 2:36–37).

- Paul fasted and prayed, and God used him to advance the gospel throughout the world (2 Corinthians 11:27).

JC had made a graph listing the names, length of fast, and prayer, followed by the results of the fast. To her surprise, she saw the revelation of a spiritual cleansing that occurred and the results of God's restoration extended to a people. The more she reviewed her information, the more questions rose. She began to see how God had created an avenue of strength as she survived her struggles through prayer and fasting. She also wanted to see if God was working on a national level to restore people or nations to Him. She listened and heard the words that sparked her interest. She decided to rewrite the information so she could have a deeper sense of what she heard. She wrote,

> Father, I am gaining a better understanding of Your process of prayer and fasting. Please share what might be a cleansing process in today's society and what You want from Your people. I see America in the news. I see the country facing natural disasters that are causing much damage. What is going on?

JC felt the Spirit of God saying these tough words of love,

> JC, I am bringing this nation, America, to her knees before Me. What I want is a repentant heart from My people so lives can be changed and saved. When My people who are called by My Name humble themselves, then I, Jehovah, will hear from heaven and heal the land. I want those who know Me to become desperate for Me, to hunger for Me, and to treat Me as I am—the only God, righteous, holy upon My Throne. My people are upon My heart. I want them to know Me intimately, to love and worship Me. They must repent of their sins and humble themselves before Me. How can the lost be reached if My people look like the lost? In order to cleanse the land, I must cleanse the church so I can draw all people to Me. My church is asleep—they play the harlot before Me. They engage in spiritual adultery which makes Me sick! I will not tolerate sin out of My people. I am God, who will not coddle nor toy with sin, for I hate it! My people should not play the harlot before Me! I see leaders delve into all kinds of ungodly acts all

in the name of My Son. Those who practice spiritual harlotry and adulterous behavior will see hell, for those individuals never knew Me. Remember My words—If My people who are called by My name will humble [fast unto Me] themselves, and pray and seek My face, and turn from their wicked ways, then I will hear from heaven, and will forgive their sin, and heal their land (2 Chronicles 7:14).

The message was clear, and JC realized it was important to pause and search her heart once again. She began to examine herself, repent of any sin, and thank Jesus for His blood that was shed for her. She sang with great joy, "O the precious blood of the Lamb!" Immediately, her soul was quieted by the presence of God. He shared how He wanted His people to change because it cost Him something when they acted like the world. The message was plain—the unsaved have no reason to see a need for a Savior, because His own people act wickedly. Without question, God wants His people to serve as His hands, feet, and mouth to a dying, lost world. His own, those who have accepted Jesus Christ as Lord and Savior, present His Son to others as they represent God the Father.

JC ended this note with what she gleaned to be the most critical lesson of surviving through prayer and fasting. She scribbled these words in red ink.

God is:

- speaking directly to those who are called by His Name (the saved);
- seeking a repentant heart;
- calling for a national fast through His church, calling us to humble ourselves before Him;

- desiring love, worship, and respect from His people; and
- reminding His people of our true calling upon this earth, which is to seek and save the lost, which is our kingdom mission.

As she closed her journal and put her pen down, she smiled and declared she knew who was in control once and for all: Jesus! At that point, she realized it was time for her to get busy with her chores. As she rose from the table, she knocked over several journals. She began to pick them up to put them in some kind of order, only to find herself laughing at a couple of pages that had yellow and red sticky notes attached to them. In her mind, she could hear herself saying, "Another eye opener!" She placed those pages on the top of the stack so she could read them the first chance she got. She glanced to see what might have sparked her to put so many sticky notes on pages and why the heavy ink marks on the paper. She promised to return immediately after her chores so she could put her curiosity to rest.

Settling Who's in Control Once and For All

The main thought of settling who's in control once and for all was seen in the next section of JC's journal. The opening lines to the entry in her journal were words she knew came from reading God's Word. She just never grasped the entire concept of giving as God so desired she would. She could tell in her writings God was using the principle of tithing to demonstrate His love and to teach her the importance of giving to Him as a means of trusting and obeying. JC thought it would be good to read slowing in order to grasp their full meaning. After the initial encounter of learning to be a consistent giver to God, she valued the new understanding of what God would do for His children when they obeyed Him.

JC read.

> I especially enjoy the way singers put Scripture into lyrics and sing the words of the Lord back to Him. One such song that keeps coming to mind is the song "Trust and Obey." The familiar words ring in my mind as I sense You leading me to trust You and obey. This is such an overwhelming feeling to say I trust You, and I want to have an obedient heart. Please tell me what You want from me? I know I give to You, but what is it You want?

JC continued to read and was amazed as she watched an element of trust emerge on the page. She paused as she began to see God requesting her to give everything in the family's checking account. She continued reading.

> I hear You telling me to go withdraw the money in our checking account. Lord, we only have seven hundred dollars to pay bills and make it to the next payday. How can You want me to give all we have in the checking account? But if that is what You want, I will go to the bank, withdraw the cash, put it in a tithing envelope and place it in the offering plate on Sunday.

JC turned the pages to find out what had transpired over those next couple of days. She saw where she had followed God's prompting, and then she read the words that she'd heard God saying to her. They had drawn her into another level of truly trusting God. "It took a lot for you to trust Me. I have cared for you. Stand on My Word. I have delivered you!"

The word the Lord had revealed to JC was found in Haggai 2:8, "The silver is Mine, and the gold is Mine," and in Psalm 50:10, 12, "For every beast of the forest is Mine, and the cattle on a thousand hills.... For the world is Mine, and all its fullness." Even in the midst of the teaching on tithing, JC had received daily instructions God expected her to follow. As things got really uncomfortable, she would become tense but learned to do what she was told to do. Part of the problem was she could not see the outcome of the things God had commanded her to do, especially since she thought some things made no sense. But during the time when the Father was dealing with her over the issue of obedience and trust, she sensed Him teaching her about Him as the God who sees all things. She learned God was revealing Himself as El

Roi, the God who sees. She quickly heard the Father share she needed to remember where He sits, what He sees, and what He knows as Almighty God. Once He quickened His identity in her spirit, she knew she had to obey Him at all cost.

To make sure she understood, the Father used one of her early morning quiet times to show her what occurred to His chosen nation when they displayed a behavior displeasing to Him. She read where the Israelites had complained and refused to obey God. She read how they did not trust or obey God and how He had referred to them as a stiff-necked, obstinate people before Him. As she read the chapter, she heard the still small voice of God saying, "Continue to read!" As she read, fear came over her. When she had finished the chapter, the Father said, "Do I have to do to you what I did to My children, Israel?" She softly said, "No, Lord." Then she heard, "Then obey and trust Me in all things without complaining—no matter what I ask you to do."

JC continued to read and saw where she had written she knew at that point God was in total control of their relationship, and He had no problem disciplining her if and when she disobeyed Him. She understood obedience to be very dear to the heart of God and He would tell her occasionally when she had grown in the area of obedience. She realized disobedience hurt the heart of God and when His children disobey, He has to deal with the sin and restore one into a right relationship with Him again. Therefore, JC prayed to have an obedient heart so she would be able to maintain a right relationship with God and avoid discipline. She was not a fan of being disciplined by God—she knew the pain that came from disobedience. She also pledged to trust Him because she wanted the security that came from following the leading of the Father.

JC read the last page and as she did, she felt an overwhelming joy fill her soul. She read how the face-to-face encounter occurred. She also read that the trials and tribulations will come, but she was to know God loved her and had all things under control. She took a deep breath as she read the words, "stripped, separated, surrendered, survived, and settled about who's in control." She heard herself reading the last line in this section of the journal.

It is important the Teacher has His way as one passes through the wilderness of life. In the process, one becomes mature in and before the Lord, for it is in the journey where one sees how the Lord God carries you, just as a man carries his sons (Deuteronomy 1:31).

STEP TWO

Identify the process of being molded—the process of change!

Jeremiah 18:6 states, "'Can I not do with you as this potter does?' says the Lord. 'Look, as the clay is in the potter's hand, so are you in My hand, ...' " The key to putting God first is to identify the process of change by knowing that it begins internally and the results of change emerge externally.

Take a few minutes to reflect over these three sections to stimulate your thinking.

Word Study: strip, separate, surrender, survive, and settle

1. _____ means to remove all excess detail; to reduce to essentials.
2. To set or keep apart or disunite means to _____.
3. _____ means to relinquish possession or control of to another; to give up or resign.
4. To carry on despite hardships or trauma; to preserve means to _____.
5. To stabilize or put in order on a permanent basis is to _____ something.

Questions:

1. In your daily journaling, what have noticed about yourself? What emotions seem to be dictating your thought processes?

2. What things do you believe God is stripping off your life? What do you believe God is asking you to give up for His greater work?

3. How do you see Him building you or molding you into the person He desires?

Tips:

1. Get through the process of the initial change with the end in mind.

2. Write a personal vision and mission statement as you take inventory of your life.

3. Recite positive affirmations each morning and throughout the day. Include affirmations related to your spiritual, physical, educational, and financial focus.

SECTION 3

Developing a Relationship: The Secret of Intimacy

The memories of the wilderness journey had left a favorable impression on JC. Nothing could prepare her for the change that would allow her to hold dear secrets in her heart. Little by little, a smile appeared on her face as she recalled the night she and her husband joined a marriage and family class. She remembered writing her name on a sheet of paper and placing it in a basket along with the rest of the class. Before the class actually started, the leaders drew names and gave away prizes. As she sat and waited to see who would win something, JC was consumed with a feeling that for the first time, her name would be called. To her surprise, the minister's wife placed her hand in the basket, and a ticket fell on the floor. The pastor urged his wife to let that ticket be the first prize given, since it seemed the ticket jumped out of the basket.

Oh, yes, the name called, of course, was JC's and to her surprise, she heard herself say aloud, "Finally, I won something!" Such amazement covered JC's face—a book was held in the air entitled, *Drawing Closer*. As she moved into the aisle to retrieve the book, she blurted out, "God must be trying to tell me something!" The entire group laughed as JC thanked the hosts and returned to her seat.

The little still voice JC had grown accustomed to hearing spoke, and she realized that, of course, He was telling her something of great value.

The Will to Know

JC entered her player room and picked up the book off the table she had received from the marriage and family class. She thumbed through the pages to see the highlights and words written on paper that conveyed her desire to know more about intimacy as outlined in the book she had received at the marriage and family class. She asked herself why this topic was so important to God and what it had to do with one drawing closer. She glanced at her writings and read.

> I am anxious to read this book because it begins with the word *intimacy*, and I think I have come into an intimate relationship with God. But maybe there is something I am missing. As I read, I wonder why and how one becomes intimate with the Father? Where am I in my walk with Him as far as intimacy is concerned? Hopefully, I will find answers to my questions as I read this book and review my notes.

After JC read several notes she had written in the book, she began to search her journal according to the notes she made in the book. She knew she had seen entries in her journal that addressed a level of intimacy with God. She turned to the journal marked, "Whose I am and whose I'm not," followed by "Drawing Closer: A New Level of Love." As she read, she heard herself say, "I never stopped to examine the pattern flow of the daily talks I had with God, or perhaps I should say the daily talks He had with me. As I read these words, I must say I have to pay more attention to the words given—they all are important because they are the heart of God to me. Now I get it! All throughout this experience, God is making sure I understand who He is and who I am in Him."

JC chose to reread her notes and rewrite words that appeared to describe who God is and who she was in Him. Before she could turn the page, she saw a note that said, "The most familiar words shared in this entry are, 'My child' followed by the Father calling me by my name, JC." She saw words such as *anointed* and *powerful person of God, priest, minister, intercessor, righteousness of God, friend*, and *My chosen and broken vessel*.

She read aloud the words that had initially shaped her view of God as her Father in heaven.

> I find a significant bonding is occurring with God the Father because He is revealing I am His child. I keep reading Ephesians 6:1–4, even though it refers to an earthly parent. I am learning God wants His children to display an attitude of obedience that honors Him.

JC continued to read how God the Father dealt with His children, Israel. She read how He basically cared, protected, and loved them unconditionally throughout the wilderness experience, how He made promises to them and showered them with blessings that seem incomprehensible to the natural eye, and how He continued to mold His children for His greater glory. She paused to think of how all she read should remind everyone that we are a reflection of Him because He made us in His image, according to His likeness (Genesis 1:26–27). This type of relationship proved to be one that caused JC to always remember since she was a child of God, it was His responsibility to care for her. She considered the stages a child goes through: birth to child, child to preteen, preteen to teenager, teenager to young adult, and young adult to mature adult. She thought of the great responsibility a parent has as the one who trains up a child in the way he should go (Proverbs 22:6) in order to learn the things of God.

She reflected upon the words that occupied her thought process. She heard, "My Child, I am preparing you for My Son!" Her words sprang from her mouth as quickly as they entered her mind. "What an awesome insight one can have knowing the Father of Creation would take time to become so intimate with the details of one's life." In the time she spent reviewing her notes, she began to understand what God wanted in an intimate relationship with her because the next word she saw was *critical.* What was so critical during that time that she had to write the word in capital letters? To her astonishment, she saw words that conveyed she had learned to hear God's voice and to realize He was a personal God who knew her name. She recited the words for the pure enjoyment of basking in His presence.

> JC, write My words: "I knew you before you were born. I have placed everything in you so you would serve and worship Me, for you are dear to My heart and I love you. Everything you are and will be is because I have created you for My great pleasure. All I plan to do with you is to bring Me honor and glory."

JC chose to write her thoughts as she reflected over the information. She saw the One who was the Creator, Weaver, Designer, and Engraver of life. For the first time, she grasped the concept of how the Father revealed who she was in Him. She saw His words as action words making her an intricate part of His work in creation. She could visualize how God was determined to use her for His work. She was already experiencing a change in her approach to serving Him because in everything she did, she found herself returning to the cross of Jesus and seeking greater revelation of the plan of redemption for mankind.

It was important at this point for JC to search for words that described God the Father. As she scanned over her writings, quickly turning pages in her journal, she saw the words, "I AM that I AM—I am Jehovah!" She read how she'd lay prostrate whenever she heard the commanding voice of authority hovering over her. This identity of God was followed by these words, "In times of storms, I am your deliver, victor, peace, restorer, healer, provider, strength, and sustainer. Seek My face always."

JC could see there were pages upon pages of information with names, titles, and Scripture references. She skipped several pages attempting to find the end of the section. She read as quickly as she could, only to find words underlined in red ink. She read the words, "Whose I will never be." She realized she had missed key passages, so she decided to take her time to reread the pages. As she began, she saw a list of words with a title stating, "His Face—Genesis, the Beginning." JC wondered if the words on the pages had the same level of excitement as they did when she first searched to know what it meant to seek the face of God.

She pondered over the words as she imagined what each word represented and meant to one with a heart searching to know God. *Compassionate, love, faithful, true* were words she whispered softly. She reminisced over the love she had felt when the Father revealed Himself in the first chapters of Genesis. She found herself thinking of the first recording of the words that revealed God's face. With a twinkle in her eye, she quietly stated, "Your face O' Lord is beautiful because your love is so pure and true..

She continued to read. On this day, I have the privilege to revisit words written in my journal that help me understand about seeking God's face. I know no man can see His face, but the thought He wants my face turned toward His glowing love at all times, helps me seek His desires. So as I seek His face, the bible reveals He is Abba Father, abiding, able, abounding, abundant, alive forevermore, all and almighty God, El Shaddai (Genesis 17:1). He enlightens my mind to know Him as zealous Zion's righteous king. His message is He has always existed and will always exist. Every name and title I read is found in His Word. I realize I cannot be what God isn't, simply because He has made me in His image. I am learning God allows people to be kings over kingdoms because He is the ultimate King and He has established His kingdom. He is King of kings and Lord of lords (1 Timothy 6:15). He is also priest (Hebrews 5:6), therefore His children are called priests unto Him (1 Peter 2:9). He is holy and has declared His children holy (1 Peter 1:16). During this intimate time, the Father and His love help me to walk with Him and trust Him when dark days hover over me. One of the special things I have come to enjoy on this journey is the way the Father shows Himself as a warrior. He continues to share His message of love as He teaches me to guard my heart and self against the attacks of the enemy. Through dreams and visions, He teaches the importance of calling on His Son who is Lord, and the defender who rescues me from every attack of Satan. The Father shares the significance of praise and worship as tools to defeat the enemy. What power occurs as the Father brings Psalm 91 to mind. He teaches me to remain in the shadow of the Almighty. The "shadow of the Almighty" is none other than Jesus Himself. As I turn the page, words emerge that truly are a revelation. The words are a powerful glimpse of God as the ultimate and sovereign Lord who reigns over the heavens and universe. Never before have I seen these words that are so powerful and remind me of whose I never will be. Out of the goodness of the Father's heart and His love for me, He reveals who the enemy is and what he is like. The Father uses several Scriptures to aid me in understanding His role as supreme God. He shares insight to His ability to create a beginning in His love. He demonstrates His greatness as a warrior who dethrones the enemy and guides me in His love.

JC wanted to reflect on her understanding of the Scriptures because she knew it was vital to her growth at that moment. t. She turned to Isaiah 14:12–14 and reread the description that portrayed Lucifer as the son of the morning. Then she turned to Ezekiel 28:13–15, that disclosed the beauty and position of Lucifer. The words of God jumped off the pages as she realized Lucifer must have been the worship leader in heaven. She read that Lucifer was in Eden, the garden of God and every precious stone was his covering: ruby, topaz, diamond, beryl, onyx, jasper, the lapis lazuli, turquoise, emerald, and gold. She saw where the Lord stated that the workmanship of Lucifer's timbrels and pipes () were in him. The Scriptures revealed Lucifer was an anointed cherub who was on the holy mountain of God and had the privilege of walking back and forth in the midst of fiery stones. God stated that Lucifer was perfect in his ways from the day he was <u>created</u> until iniquity was found in him. Then she turned back to Isaiah 14, where she read verses 13 and 14, which revealed Lucifer wanted to ascend into heaven and exalt his throne above the stars of God. The declaration he made was that he would sit on the mount of the congregation in the farthest sides of the north and ascend above the heights of the clouds to be *like* the Most High.

JC examined her journal to see what other Scriptures had been listed. She found Revelation 12:9 and she read it slowly, finding that it described war in heaven. It became apparent that a name change had occurred for Lucifer. She saw the word of God state that the "great dragon was cast out, the serpent of old who is called the devil and Satan, who deceives the whole world. He was cast out to the earth and his angels were cast out with him." The power of this Scripture allowed JC to see the warrior God, who kicked Lucifer out of heaven. Since Lucifer could not dethrone God, he then chose to mess with God's children by becoming a thief who steals, kills, and destroys (John 10:10). He sends fiery darts against the child of God (Ephesians 6:16). The thought of destroying the children of God with poisoned darts (temptations and events that challenge one's walk) or forces of darkness (pride, rebellion, lust, greed, self-righteousness, guilt, anger, and hatred, just to name a few) so they miss the purpose of their existence on earth has continued from generation to generation. JC stopped and stated loudly, "The enemy cares nothing for the soul of man!" In all she read, God shared she did not belong to the enemy nor was she to be a toy in his hands. At that point, she returned to her journal, finding the last page of the section. She found three points highlighted in yellow and decided to write them down again and pray for the souls of mankind. It was important she pray because of what she had learned about the plans of the enemy. The enemy, she wrote, attempts to do three things:

- cause pain and misfortune in the lives of God's children;
- blind the minds and hearts of God's children, encouraging them to seek and worship idols instead of God alone; and
- blind the minds of everyone who is not a child of God to keep them from seeing Christ as Lord and Savior who has prepared a place for them in heaven.

It seemed like hours passed as JC prayed for souls. She prayed and thanked the Father He was able to guide her into His limitless love as He taught her she would never belong to the enemy of her soul because of the great price He gave to purchase her soul. She continued to thank God for crushing the enemies of her soul as she spent time reciting words of encouragement to herself. She vowed to pursue God who was righteous and holy and who taught her to have faith, demonstrate love, and persevere in all things. As she lay prostrate on the floor, the threshing floor, where God had taught her to practice the presence of His Son, she began to call on Jesus who was her advocate, high priest, mediator, propitiation for sins, redeemer and the resurrection and the life for all eternity. She began to praise God for who He is and declare He alone was worthy of praise. At the moment, the will to know and become intimate with the Father had taken hold. JC knew she had entered into a new level of love because God had her right where He wanted her; in the palms of His loving hands—close to His heart!

Drawing Closer: A New Level of Love

The difficulty of grasping a loving relationship with someone you have never seen can be an anxious time, and so it was for JC as she worked to comprehend the concept of the new level of love ingrained in her heart. In an attempt to understand the magnitude of this love affair—the courtship, pursuit, union, wedding day, and marriage (consummation)—she reflected on the experience she had had with the man who became her husband. She remembered the courtship, the pursuit, but more so the wedding day. As she recalled that day, she thought of how everything proceeded as planned. The music was right, flower girls and attendants were in place, and the parents and guests displayed laughter and joy. But mostly what JC remembered was the excitement she'd had as she walked down the aisle to see the one who had stolen her heart, the most handsome man in the world, wearing a beautiful tuxedo. She remembered her dress and the train that covered the aisle and brought a newness that could only portray grace and elegance. Her heart began to race once again as joyful memories lingered in her mind.

She wandered off in thought to the description she had seen in the Bible of a wedding between the Bridegroom and His bride. JC quickly turned to the Scriptures that revealed the New Jerusalem as the bride of Christ. The narrative found in Revelation 21:2 and 9 described the city prepared as a bride adorned for her husband. The words *bridegroom* and *husband* were vital to her understanding the role of the husband in an intimate relationship as God saw it. She turned to Hosea 2, which served as a reference to understanding what the Word of God said about who He was to the nation of Israel. She went on to read an account of how God betrothed His people. In the midst of things, JC decided to reread those Scriptures so she could see the detailed intimacy of how the pursuit occurred by the wooing of the Father for a nation, a people. Excitement penetrated her soul as she read with enthusiasm the Scriptures pertaining to the love affair God had with Israel—and now was offering her.

> "And it shall be in that day,' says the Lord, 'that you will call Me My Husband and no longer call me, My Master.... I will betroth you to Me forever; Yes, I will betroth you to Me in righteousness and justice, in loving-kindness and mercy, and I will betroth you to Me in faithfulness.' " (Hosea 2:16, 19–20).

JC felt the warmth that had invaded her heart on many occasions. She knew it was one more step of the all-sufficient God to share His love and devotion with her. She sensed Him saying, "I will be right, just, merciful, compassionate, and faithful as your Husband and Maker. Simply respond as a wife who will submit, present, and offer yourself totally to Me." JC realized the wooing process never ends because the Father is always pursuing His people with an everlasting love as He cares, defends, protects, and delivers them from all things. She saw Him as the El Olam, the eternal, everlasting One (Isaiah 26:4; Psalm 90:2), who captures the whole heart as He moves in to His rightful place as head, always having preeminence in everything (Colossians 1:18).

Words that surfaced in her mind at this time were those of encouragement, security, safety, and closeness. She thought how Jesus had always been her friend and how He had guided her into an intimate relationship as He displayed an unconditional and incomprehensible love for her. She recognized the union began the day she accepted Christ as her Savior and realized the magnitude of Him hanging on the cross securing her salvation for eternity. She thought of a sermon she had heard about intimate friends. She began to understand Christ Jesus draws people into an inner circle as He makes known the secrets of the Father's heart, full of love for His children.

JC began to scan through her journal to find any information pertaining to the friendship of Christ. Instead, she found the notes from that sermon about friendship. As she read, she was amazed at the details of the relationship Christ had with three of His disciples.

Jesus had many disciples (Luke 10) but the first twelve disciples He selected (Matthew 10:1) traveled with Him upon the earth during His ministry. All twelve of them saw Him heal and feed the lost. He gave power to all twelve to do as the Father so desired. But only three were at the transfiguration (Luke 9:28–36) and at the garden of Gethsemane (Mark 14:32–42). All went to the mountain, but only three were invited to continue up the mountain. Jesus only took three to Gethsemane with Him. It was the same three that went up the mountain with Him. Jesus loved them all but only three—Peter, James and John—chose to become intimate with Jesus, and thus His inner circle was formed. They knew Jesus. They knew his strengths, concerns, and challenges. They knew His desires and joys.

During the stay in the garden of Gethsemane, the Scripture tells how Jesus began to be very distressed and troubled, and He told them His soul was deeply grieved to the point of death. He also told His friends to remain there, to keep watch, and to pray. Only an intimate friend reveals the depths of the soul, his heart. He trusted them with the very secrets of His soul. Then at the transfiguration, Peter, James, and John were afforded the opportunity to have a glimpse of Jesus in His full glory, the Son of God, the Lord and Savior, King, Priest and Master, and to hear the voice of God letting them know Jesus is the Son of God, the chosen One, and they were to listen to Him (Luke 9:35).

JC understood Jesus does not have favorites but affords everyone the opportunity to become intimate with Him. Those disciples who were intimate with Jesus chose to get closer to Him because of their genuine love and desire to know Him, all of Him. At that point, she became aware of the fact that to know and want to know more about Jesus was the secret to a new level of love. The more one learned about the love of God the Father and how He withholds nothing from a person, the more one can get into the inner circle by baring the soul, obeying His every commandment, and loving Christ unconditionally.

JC grasped the concept—the deeper she fell in love with the Father through her Savior and friend Jesus, the more she would be able to love her family and friends unconditionally, love those who hurt her, and forgive anyone who mistreated her. She learned the value of drawing close to the Father and staying in the safe place through praise and worship.

Her ability to remember the love affair began at the cross of Calvary, where her ultimate responsiveness to a loving relationship formed. She knew the heart of God met hers as a bridegroom meets His bride, and she gave herself to Him intimately for all eternity.

She found the greatest joy and peace as she understood it was important to ask Him to teach her who she was in Him and to shower her in His love while always telling Him she loved Him. Thus, JC found the new level of love based in an unconditional acceptance and respect for herself—the very thing she had longed for—and now she knew how to love God and man.

STEP THREE

Identify the breakdown of a lack of love in your life. Seek healing through agape love, for it yields great fruit!

1 John 4:19 states, "We love Him because He first loved us." The key learning here is to identify God's love in our life and how He teaches us to love Him, as well as others.

Take a few minutes to reflect over these three sections to stimulate your thinking.

Word Study: intimacy, love, conditional, and unconditional

1. _____ is a deep, tender, ineffable feeling of affection toward a person. The expression of one's affection.
2. _____ love is imposing, dependent, or containing a grip on a person. The restrictive acceptance of a person. Placing limits on a relationship based on the standards defined by a person.
3. The absolute acceptance of a person without conditions or limitations is _____
4. The act of being very personal, private, and being in a position to display an innermost affection with someone is defined as _____.

Questions:

1. When did you experience a lack of love in your life?
2. Whose love did you desire and did not/could not receive? Why?
3. What signs are visible in your life that you display conditional love for your family or friends? What keeps you from displaying unconditional love to yourself, family, friends, even your enemies?
4. How has God expressed His unconditional love to you and through you?

Tips:

1. Even if it is hard, take the painful look into your past to determine what has caused you to be wounded and find it difficult to love as Christ desires.
2. Make a list and share it with God, all the while taking the painstaking event(s) to the cross of Christ. Leave it there and never pick it up again.
3. Find Scriptures of love and recite those daily. Tell your loved ones that you truly love them and work toward accepting yourself unconditionally as you also move to accept your loved ones unconditionally.

SECTION 4

A Hunger and a Thirst

An overwhelming feeling emerged in JC's soul that caused her to hunger and thirst for God in a new way. She wanted to experience Him at a level that would cause her to dig deeper into His Word and gain an understanding of all she was reading. In the midst of all she experienced, JC found herself thinking of Him every moment of the day. She knew that, in order to have an encounter with God like never before, she had to put her heart, mind, and soul into action as she sought the very presence of God.

To gain a deeper walk with God, JC used the approach of asking Him the questions that stirred her soul. She began to write words that came to mind about the heart of God, about His thoughts and voice. She vowed to begin her search, of course, at the beginning—Genesis. Her goal was to move across the pages of the Bible from Genesis to Revelation, seeking the very phrases that described the heart of God, His mindset, words used to depict His ways—she sought the very image of who He was.

The revelation of there being no God except Jehovah led JC into a deeper quest to know the One who declared, "I am the Lord, and there is no other; there is no God besides Me." (Isaiah 45:5). Just in those words alone, JC realized searching for His heart would be a monumental task, but one that would lead to great gains. Thus the hunger and thirst led to a vast communion, conversation, and confirmation with the One who is known as "I AM."

THE HEART OF GOD

Weeks passed before JC entered her little room again to read from her journals. She spent most of her time completing a Bible study course from her church. The class was one that required her to focus on one main book of the Bible and work on a project that would reflect a major theme from the book. JC had begun to understand how to study the Bible and to gain insight to the themes that emerged. She was finding key applications for daily living.

While she enjoyed the class and the major points from the text, she wanted to know more about the book's author and content As she entered her little room, she carried several books written by Bible scholars and ministers of the Word of God so she could engage in a comprehensive review of the book studied by her class. Since she had to complete a project, she decided to entitle the lesson, "Touching the Heart of God," because of what she had gathered from reading different commentaries. She continued to ask how someone could touch the heart of God. She attempted to narrow her topic to a focus on prayer, but in her notes the same question seemed to emerge: "What does the heart of God look like in order for someone to touch His heart?"

In her journals there was always the message of love, but never could she remember a solid indication she knew the *heart* of God. She wondered if it was possible for anyone to truly know the heart of God.

From that thought, the flame of a new quest surfaced—one she would pursue until some answer emerged.

Days later, JC found herself at her table with paper and pen in hand. She made an outline as to how she would approach this topic and, of course, her approach always led her to see what information might be found in her journal; but where would she begin? With her Bible opened to the book of Genesis, she began to read to see if she might find words that would give insight to the heart of God.

JC had discovered reading the Bible aloud was one way she could communicate with God as well as allow her to focus on what she read. So she began reading aloud. "Genesis 1:1, 'In the beginning God created....' " She continued to read and make notes so she could recount her words. She decided taping her reflections would allow her to hear as well as examine the words that might give insight into the heart of God. After several hours, she played the tape to gain insight to the knowledge acquired. Excitement filled her heart as she heard such wonderful expressions.

> In the first couple of chapters of Genesis, I see words such as *blessed, faithful, forgiving, fruitful, giving, good, gracious, helping, holy, jealous, joyful, peaceful, purposeful, protective, revealing* and *sorrowful.* So far the Scriptures reveal God has a brave, caring, compassionate, complete, courageous, devoted, gentle, glad, humble, just, loving, merciful, patient, passionate, perfect, pure, receiving, righteous, sacrificial, sharing, sincere, thankful, truthful, understanding, and victorious heart. As I record this information, I get the distinct feeling the Father is saying there is no way to know the depths of His heart. What I do know is He reveals in His Word

that "out of the abundance of the heart the mouth speaks" (Matthew 12:34); therefore, His heart speaks all that is good, pure, and right because He is His Word.

JC began to record her thoughts and questions on a separate sheet of paper as she continued to read. She wrote:

Before I can understand the heart of God (as though that were possible), I must know what the heart is. In *Vine's Expository Dictionary*, I see the word for heart is "leb labe" which refers to the heart, mind, and midst. It can refer to the organ of the body, the inner part or middle of a thing, or the seat of emotions, knowledge, and wisdom. So the only way man can experience God's heart is when the Father speaks out of His mouth to declare His heart. The heart of God is manifested through what He proclaims about Himself and what He says He will do. In Jeremiah 3:15, the Father tells His people He will give them shepherds according to His heart, who will feed them on knowledge and understanding. What is knowledge and understanding except the revelation of who He is as revealed through His heart?

As JC continued to study what she had written, she began to see how, in her relationship with the Father, she had often asked Him to engulf her heart into His. She saw this request emerge as she moved from being a pessimist to learning how to accept and give love. She experienced fellowship with the Father, and in so doing, it became imperative to examine her own heart before God. The examination required a continual cutting away of layers of hurt, pain, and distrust that could only be removed by studying the Word of God. JC had come to the point where she gave her heart to God daily, so she would be in a position to know more about His heart. It was in the search to know God's heart that she saw for the first time how dark man's heart really was.

In Genesis 8:21, JC found that the imagination of man's heart was evil from his youth, and in Genesis 6:5, she read that the wickedness of man was great in the earth, and that every intent of man's thoughts of his heart was only evil continually. She began to realize that the things [words] that proceed out of the mouth of man came from his very heart, and man's words are what defile him. As she completed her word search pertaining to the heart of man, she read the list of things God indicated proceed out of the heart of man; things such as evil thoughts, murders, adulteries, fornications, thefts, false witness, and blasphemies (Matthew 15:18–19). She quickly understood the transformation in her life came because the Father had been teaching her about establishing a right relationship with Him through a daily communion of displaying a repentant heart, one being refined and molded in His hands.

JC scanned through a couple more journals to see what other words or messages she could find on the topic. As she read, she could see a hunger for God in her words, and she understood her heavenly Father had chosen to share His thoughts with her. His powerful voice echoed in her ear.

> "JC, I will let you find Me and know My heart. What you have seen in My Word is My heart. My voice will guide you through any wilderness as well as any search for who I am. When you yield yourself to Me, I begin to change your heart at a deeper level by sharing who I

am as I pour My love over you. In all you do, obey Me
as I reveal Myself to you."

At that moment, JC began to thank God for allowing her to see a
glimpse of His heart upon the pages of His Word. Previously, during the
times she read her Bible, she had not understood she was seeing God's
heart. She continued to read a few more pages of her journal to see if
His heart appeared in her writings—now that she knew what to look
for. She understood a spiritual union, a unity of hearts materialized as
the lover of her soul radiated His holiness and glory over her very being.
Understanding God reveals His heart through His Word and presence
caused JC to thirst for more of Him.

The presence was an indescribable calmness or stillness that emitted
unspeakable joy. It was in the remaining hours of the day that she cried
out unto the Lord to let her heart rejoice in seeking Him and give Him
the praise due His glorious Name. In a moment's time, it dawned on
her His presence was the safe place and it allowed her to commune with
the Father at all times because her heart was being trained to be like His
Son's: pure, clean, and holy. It was His tender leading JC sensed as she
was being trained to stay focused on Him. In her conversations with
Him, she understood her learning swept her into another dimension
that involved the mind of Christ.

THE HEAD OF GOD

The words *mind of Christ* rang in JC's head for days. She had completed several book studies on the mind of Christ but could not fathom what she was being led to gather from this constant pending thought referencing the mind of Christ. What she did know was her heart belonged to the Father, and her revelation of His heart upon the pages of His Word proved God's heart was tender, gentle, and responsive to man.

She decided to review her course study books, and as she did, she found the study provided insight to the Scriptures that conveyed an understanding of the mind of Christ. What JC remembered as she studied the lesson and the Scriptures that led her to reshape her thinking and caused her to seek to obey God, was a great revelation i gained as He had told her to stay focused on Him.

Her awareness was monumental as the Father taught her His heart and mind were one, just like He, His Son, and Spirit were One. She reviewed her notes in the outline of the text and began to see every entry had a reminder that the mind was the battleground and if unprotected, all sorts of filth would filter through, causing one to get trapped in the world of doubt, unbelief, mistrust, and disobedience. In a section labeled "Who's occupying your mind," JC saw the transition on the pages of the booklet where she'd practiced stating 1 Corinthians 2:16, which focused on the mind of Christ. In her continuous recitation of the Scripture, she felt a strength drawing her to have confidence in the

Word of God. She saw she had written a message she knew came from God, and which made more sense to her now. She read,

> During any journey, it is important to keep your eyes on the lover of your soul. It is important to capture every thought and bring it under the authority of My Son, Jesus. As you keep your mind on Him, you will know peace, My perfect peace. As I test your mind and search your heart, know I will bring you into the peace I so desire. I am the One who has put wisdom in your mind and given you understanding of heart so you can see what a sound mind and pure heart resembles. I need you to know that a mind that is steadfast on Me is the type of mind I need you to have; therefore I want you to love Me with all your mind. During your journey, I want you to have a willing and calm mind before Me. Guard your heart and mind as I renew you each day and night. Read My Word and gird your loins with My laws. As you read My Word, you will know My heart for you and My *will* shall come forth in your life.

By the end of the section on "Who's occupying your mind," JC understood the goal of the Father was to assist her in truly understanding if her mind was on fleshly things, she could not please Him (Romans 8:8). But if her mind stayed steadfast on the Father, she would know His will as she walked daily in His peace, no matter what transpired. As JC continued to scan through the booklet, her notes became a treasured item because she saw repetitive words that became specific to her walk. She even found reviewing the phrases brought a rejuvenating zest to her time of reflection. She rewrote the phrases and labeled them as the will of God based on His heart and mind. She knew God's will for her was to:

- fear the Lord (fear displayed as an awesome reverence for Him);
- walk in all His ways;
- love Him with a whole heart, mind, and soul;
- serve Him with all her heart;
- seek Him and learn all she could about and from Him;
- present her body a living and holy sacrifice, acceptable unto God;
- be transformed by the renewing of her mind;
- worship, believe, and trust Him; and
- obey Him in all things.

As she continued to read, she heard the sweet, gentle voice saying, "Write!" At that moment, she opened her journal and began to write.

> Write these words in order and as you search their meaning—*covenant* (agreement), *commandments* (instruction), *conversations* (two-way, audible/speaking, face-to-face), *communion* (intimacy, close association, relationship), *commitments* (vow, pledge, obligation) and *consecration* (sanctification, dedication, devotion), know they convey My divine will.

> After reviewing the definitions of the words, she wrote her understanding of what the Father was teaching her. She surmised that His divine will is to establish His agreement to bond (connect) with man by providing detailed instruction as He utilizes His written Word as well as His audible voice to initiate intimate two-way communication with man. He pledges to dedicate

Himself through Jesus Christ as He seeks man's devotion through obedience so He can bless man (mankind). Thus knowing His *will* should cause man to be sensitive to His leading through His Holy Spirit.

What JC realized was her level of understanding of unity found in God had grown because of her desire to know all she could about Him and His ways. She began to comprehend that the Spirit of God revealed the deep things of God and carried out the thoughts of God for the world. The earnest desire to know the Father through His heart and mind caused JC to seek the precious things of God, and the Holy Spirit ushered her into the presence of God which confirmed she was in the safe place of the Father, His heart and head.

JC backed away from the table and moved to the floor as she was compelled to lay prostrate on the floor with her hands wide open and palms opened facing heaven as she kept her mind focused on the Lord. She knew at that moment as she lay out before the Lord, she was offering herself to Him as she emptied her soul before Him, knowing her position, especially her open hands, indicated no secrets were withheld from the lover of her soul, just as He had visited her and revealed that His hands were open to her—signifying He withheld nothing from her, for He was always inviting her to come to Him and receive His love.

When JC arose from the floor, she felt a peace consuming her. She began to sing, "He's got the whole world in His hands." As she sang the old familiar words, her body swayed in union with the tune that flowed from her lips. She remembered words spoken by the Father, "I will meet you in your dance." At that moment, she began to swirl around with her hands arched as though she was in the arms of the Lord, dancing to His choreographic movements. This time it wasn't the Father whispering words of love to her, she was whispering words of love to Him. The words that came from her mouth flowed from her heart. "Thank You, my Lord, for always holding my hand in Your Hand and keeping me on Your mind. I am very appreciative of the way You have taught me about the mind of Christ and held my hand through the rough times of life. Your hand is all that is pure and good, and I am reminded no one shall snatch me out of Your hand. Your hand is Your strength and power, laced with kindness, mercy, truth, and righteousness. You are shaping me to become the person You desire for Your work and kingdom. Thank You for inscribing me in Your hands and teaching me that treasures lie in the palms of Your hands."

JC did not want the moment to end because she felt such peace at the thought of the Father receiving her words and being pleased that she wanted more—more understanding of Him and His love for mankind. She wanted to tell everyone all she had learned but knew God wanted His private intimate time to remain just that—intimate. She could only equate the encounter she experienced to the cross where Jesus hung as He was beaten, pierced, marred, bruised, suffocated, and died for all mankind. His arms were outstretched, palms up, and His blood ran freely, the picture of God's outstretched arms and hands as a reminder He withheld nothing from man. He extended His love while declaring He still hungered and thirsted for a relationship with man. He gave access to Himself through Jesus so intimate communion could occur, as He so desires.

In the remaining moments of her quiet time, JC scribbled these words—For the next generation of people, learn that *God is love and He is very tenderhearted toward His people. He desires that all come to the saving grace of Jesus Christ.* He has chosen to strive with man; therefore, pursue His heart, for He is love, mercy, goodness, and hope. He is the One who hungers and thirsts as He reaches into the very bowels of His soul to share His love for you. Remember He declares, "I AM that I AM—love!"

L–Lover of your soul

O–Omniscient, Omnipresent, Omnipotent

V–Victorious Warrior

E–Eternal King, Everlasting One

Step Four

Take inventory of yourself!

Matthew 5:6 states, "Blessed are those who hunger and thirst for righteousness, for they shall be filled." In the growth process, examine your heart and mind because Jesus says, "Everyone who thirsts, come to the waters; And you who have no money, come, buy and eat…without money and without price" (Isaiah 55:1). Be filled on the meat of the Word and drink from the fountain of living water!

Take a few minutes to reflect over these three sections to stimulate your thinking.

Word Study: heart, mind

The _____is one's innermost character, feelings, or inclinations, while the _____is the element in an individual that perceives, thinks, or reasons.

Questions:

1. In your Bible, what words do you see that describe the heart of God?

2. Describe your heart. Is there evidence your heart reflects the heart of God? If not, what can you do to align your heart with His?

3. What does the Word of God encourage you to do about your thoughts?

Tips:

1. Learn to express His heart. Learn and pray Proverbs 23:26; Jeremiah 31:3 and Psalm 103: 8, 17.

2. Memorize Scripture to develop your mind. Memorize Philippians 2:5–8 and Romans 12:1–.

3. Change your atmosphere. Pursue God through His Word.

SECTION 5

The Journey of a Lifetime

The end of one event will always move a person into another path or walk of life. So it was for JC. The internship with a prestigious school district had come to an end. She was confident and ready to advance in her profession and use the newly-acquired skills to lead a school district herself.

During the farewell luncheon, many of the leaders within the district and community presented her with gifts of appreciation. As she returned to her little office to collect her final belongings, she paused to read the inscription from a book given to her by the district level media specialist. JC had no clue the words would be a prophetic message. The words: "JC, you have been such a witness to me this year. Read this book and learn the true value of its contents—for as you leave your training ground, you will need this book to continue to shape your growth process. For in the coming days, you will be like King David, who declared he would wait in the plains of the wilderness until word came from the Lord to inform him as to what to do (2 Samuel 15:28)."

At the end of the workday, as she said her good-byes and loaded her things into her car, she could not help but think of the words read as well as the title of the book, *Waiting On God*. She knew she had grown before the Father, but now she sensed there was still another stretch He desired. What she had experienced in the journey was the Father working in her private life and now showing her what He planned to do in her professional life, but to Him it was all one walk before Him. Thus the struggle began.

LEARNING TO WAIT ON AND FOR GOD

JC did not mind staying in the community where she worked. She had come to like the quaint little town. The sun was shining and a gentle breeze filled the air. Her first interview ended with the screening committee indicating she would be the candidate recommended to the Board as their choice to lead their district. She was thankful her mentor had done everything right in training her for the interview and organization of a school district. All JC had to do was show up for the interview and present herself as the candidate of choice. The final interview would be on Monday so she decided to remain in the community over the weekend so her trip would not be a long one. She wanted to have time for herself as she prepared to meet the committee on Monday. As she drove to a hotel and parked her car, the music on the radio stopped, and a story about Naomi began. While she knew the story well, her focus had always been on the love Ruth displayed for Naomi, but this time the story highlighted the death of Naomi's husband and sons because they had left their homeland and traveled to a new land where God had not told them to go. At that point, the radio broadcast went silent.

JC heard, "Do not go into the land! Return to your home district in submission!" JC shook her head and thought to herself it was just her nerves trying to shake her or maybe the enemy trying to disrupt her plans. She checked into the hotel and proceeded to make preparations for her interview early Monday morning. As she readied herself, she made sure she had packed samples of projects she had orchestrated from her previous district. Since she was exhausted from the activities of the day, JC called it an early night and went to bed.

She was awakened by an early phone call from a friend stating people were excited she was coming back to her home district and she would be at the intermediate school as their new principal. JC laughed and stated she knew nothing about those plans because she would have completed an interview for another job on Monday and would be moving forward with what she wanted to do as a superintendent of a school district. On Wednesday she was, and at that time since she could retire, she would be submitting her retirement papers.

As she rose to enter into her quiet time she heard, "JC, don't go into the land, return to your district in submission!" JC began to sing and enter worship, but everything seemed so stale and uneventful. She attempted to write in her journal and read her Bible, but emptiness seemed to fill her soul. She began to write and exhibit boldness before God which later unfolded into brokenness as she crumbled into shattered pieces of a fragile shadow of herself.

God, I want to do what I want. I do not want to return to my home district because I believe You have prepared me to be over a district, and I want to move forward in a new way—new life. I see how things can be so much better for people, and I want what I want. Grant me my request and allow me to go to another land to work. You know I will serve You in the new land, just like You have allowed me to serve You during this internship. I have obeyed Your voice to be trained and witness to Your people. Lord, souls were saved during this time in the district and lives changed—so grant me the opportunity to move forward in a new place so I can enjoy working in the area You have prepared for me. Lord, I am not returning to land I came from!

Silence filled the room for what seemed like eternity. JC sat on the floor, believing she had moved the heart of God, but in the stillness of the moment, she sensed a strong presence and words were spoken. "JC, Moses returned, and who are you that you should not obey Me? Put your face on the ground before Me and stop whining, for I am Jehovah and I desire obedience out of My children. Do not go into the land. Return to your home district in submission—submission to Me!"

JC knew she had wrestled with God about returning to her home district and His final answer required an act of obedience filled with fear because of the sternness of His voice and presence that filled the room. She knew as she obeyed Him to put her face on the ground before Him. He meant not to accept the offer to interview as well as the job because He had closed the door. She knew God loved her enough to discipline her especially for any defiant act of disobedience. He reminded her she was not her own because she had been purchased with a great price—the blood of His Son.

She rose from the floor, broken and somewhat confused because she earnestly thought she knew what God had trained her to do and she was ready to move forward. Everything seemed to be in His right timing, but He had come to her to tell her to return to the place she left. So she packed her things, called the chairperson of the screening committee to withdraw her name, called her mentor to say she had to return to her district, and then called her husband to say she knew God was not in the placement so she would return to her previous district. With tears in her eyes and her heart broken, she checked out of the hotel and drove home to prepare for what God wanted her to do. She rode down the highway in silence. Disappointment filled her heart, but she was determined to obey even though she did not understand what was happening.

Upon her arrival home, she found a message for her to report to the intermediate school on Wednesday, and when she arrived, she was to meet with the former principal to make the transition a smooth one. \

She wrote the message in her planner and spent time sharing with her husband the events that filled that last day of her internship. She decided to spend Saturday resting as her husband worked around the house. As she walked up the stairs, JC heard the calming voice of her husband, "Things always work out in God's timing. Since you say you hear from God, take time to listen instead of petitioning Him for what you want—you know it's all about Him anyway."

JC took his words to heart and made her way around to her little room to spend time in worship. During her time in the little room which she had renamed her "Little Delight," she grabbed her journal, got in a position to listen, and asked God what He wanted her to do. The words flowed.

JC, I want you to learn to grow where I have planted you. We (the Father, Son, and Holy Spirit) have waited for you to get to this point in your walk before Us. Your desires are before Me, but what I desire is for you to wait on and for Me! What is so difficult about waiting for Me? If you love Me, you will wait on and for Me—wait on and for Me!

The conversation was over, and JC knew a decision was before her… as if she had any control over the situation. But it wasn't about control as much as it was about her love and devotion to God. So she declared at that moment she would wait for the Father especially the area of a promise He repeatedly made to her. She spent the remaining days before she reported to work reading her book so she could learn about waiting on God. She wrote whatever came to mind about waiting on and for God. She even wanted to know the difference between waiting on God and waiting for Him. As she read, she found herself experiencing a new level of peace and quietness. She even stated she enjoyed the waiting process for it was something totally new to her, and she could tell the difference in her mind-set.

Wednesday came and she reported to work. The office staff greeted her with words of encouragement and welcome to the school. The former principal immediately reviewed the basic information relating to the budget, staffing, and scheduling. At the end of the day, she received a telephone call from another principal who indicated they should have lunch to catch up on the things of the district. JC declined by stating the workload was too much and she needed to get things ready for opening day. At that point, the principal asked JC if she knew the district was without a superintendent.

JC thought to herself—this is what God has prepared for me. JC searched for the announcement pertaining to the job and immediately began to prepare her application. She completed the application and mailed it within the week. She noticed the closing date for the job was after the opening of school but felt confident God had worked out the details, so no matter what happened, He could make her transition smooth.

She interviewed a few weeks later. She had people praying and believed she was the choice for the job. The committee indicated an announcement would come the next day because they would not leave until they had made a decision. She left the interview, went home, and took time to write out her thoughts, including thanking God for His favor. As she prepared for bed, an uneasy feeling came over her. She sensed she was not the choice for the job, so she decided to pray to calm her fears.

As she arrived at work the next morning, she received a telephone call indicating she was not selected but to keep trying, for something would happen in her favor one day. She opened her journal and wrote: "Where have I missed You, Lord, and what are You doing with my life?"

Then she closed her journal and called her husband to share the news. She knew she had to hold her emotions in check and not allow her staff to see her disappointment, hurt, and pain. She walked the halls of the school and did what she knew would bring joy to her day, she hugged students and spent time listening to what they were learning in class and what was happening in their world. As she prepared to leave work, the news reached her staff, as well as friends throughout the district. She made it a point to send a congratulatory e-mail to the person selected because she needed to make sure her soul harbored no ill feelings.

She arrived home several hours before her husband, so she decided to search her journal entries to see how she had missed God. What she found were words that conveyed she was in a *waiting* process. Her mind traveled back to the inscription from the book (learn the true value of waiting on God) given to her by the media specialist. Those words of being like David who waited until word came from the Lord to inform him as to what to do, rung loudly in her mind. JC shook her head in disbelief as she released her hurt, pain, and distrust of God. She did not want any prophetic words. She had been obedient but felt betrayed by the One who had promised so many things—but the one thing she thought He had trained her for had not materialized. The only thing surfacing was this thing called waiting. She did not spend time reading because her emotions were raw. She prepared supper and realized she was not in the mood to wait for her husband, so she chose to eat and then go to bed without spending time with the Father. Matter of fact, when she rose the next morning, she didn't pray. She just prepared for work. She made a decision as she drove to work to move forward by seeking other districts that might be in the process of selecting a superintendent. She had changed her mind about waiting on God. She did not want to wait in prayer before Him, make decisions His way, or give Him time to share His thoughts. She yelled aloud in the car, "I don't want to wait any longer! I can't wait for You to teach me another lesson. I am not getting any younger and I don't want my life to be spent working late into my sixties. I want control of my life!" At that point, JC chose to keep God out of her life and do things her own way. She consciously did not pray, read, or worship the Father. Six days had passed by with no intimate time shared between the Father and JC. Of course, it was all JC's doing.

At midnight a week later, JC was awakened and drawn to meet with the Father. As she gathered her materials while displaying a begrudging demeanor, she heard the Father tell her to "Grow up!" She also heard she would bow her knee to Him and wait for and on Him. As she waited to hear more, she began to write the words that pierced her heart.

> JC, your Promised Land is delayed because you have chosen to allow your attitude and lack of trust to cloud your understanding of who I am and what I am capable of doing. You took your eyes off Me while closing Me out of your life because you believed you knew what was best for you. I did not want you in that particular land because My vision is bigger than that one job. What I want you to do is trust Me in this waiting process because it is about souls, not your own personal desires or plans for your life. I am in charge of everything, so wait on and for Me. My name is Patience, and you will succumb to what I desire for your life. I am the keeper of your soul as well as your destiny—not you!

Instantly, JC cried out and repented before Him, thanking Him because He still cared enough to let her enter into His presence by covering her in the shed blood of His Son. In His kindness and mercy, He confirmed His promise was only delayed and she would still enter the Promised Land because it was truly about the souls of people and her destiny before Him.

JC dried her tears and looked at a set of questions she had written in her moments of boldness before the Father. She petitioned the Father to respond because she had come to realize the whole life cycle of man was about waiting on and for God. In the midst of the responses, the Father stated her thought was true; the whole life cycle was about waiting on and for Him. As she prepared to hear His responses to her questions, she opened her journal, took her pen in hand, and began to write.

> JC, your first question is, what is the purpose of "free will" if people really don't have a choice where waiting on and for Me is concerned? You have a choice to wait or not. You told Me you were willing to wait for Me no matter how long it takes. You gave me your word which means something to me. Have you changed your mind? *No, Lord, I have not.* Then wait on and for Me, JC.

> Your second question is when do you grow weary of waiting? Your travail (toiling, suffering) is waiting on Me to bring forth the promises I have made to you. You want the promises which are laced blessings to emerge so you can be relieved from the things that plague your soul. You want freedom because you believe it will cure things for you. Another problem you have is that you think you know how I am going to deliver you. You want to know how and when, but that's My business. When you take your eyes off Me, you grow tired of waiting.

Joanna Cummings Washington

Your third question is what in your life has not been surrendered to Me? JC, it is not that you have not surrendered to Me, it is your impatience that surfaces when you are faced with a personal issue of how I am going to deliver you. I remind you, My name is Patience. You are learning how to abide in Me and when you truly learn how to abide, all things will come together. The two things I want you to do now are to gain understanding of the word *wait* and to learn the difference in the words *for* Me and *on* Me. Begin your search now!

JC immediately began her assignment to learn about waiting on and for God. She researched the word *wait* and found associated words such as *abide, stay, remain, linger, continue, persist, prolong, hang back,* and *stay behind*. Then she read, "Abide [remain and linger] in Me, and I in you. As the branch cannot bear fruit of itself unless it abides in the vine, neither can you, unless you abide in Me" (John 15:4). She proceeded to read John 15:1–11. There she saw how the Father wanted her to learn to abide, to wait on and for Him. If she abided (hung back, stayed behind Him), that meant she would be waiting she on and for the Father His power, strength, protection and, love to flow. From her study, she was learning to wait in prayer. She had to wait in prayer, plans, promises, and provisions.

Her next assignment was to know the difference between waiting on and waiting for the Father. Her search led her to one hundred sixty-seven references for *waiting* and at least forty alluded to waiting for God. Still, JC needed clarity of the two, so she respectfully asked the Father to share His thoughts on the difference. She learned *waiting for* the Father allowed Him to get into position, and *waiting on* the Father

110

allowed Him to answer prayer and bring the riches of His love to her. She also understood there was deliverance when one waited on Him because a person was waiting on God to deliver all He said He would.

She paused to soak it all up and take it all in. The knowledge she gained the most was God was working patience in her, and the Scriptures used to teach her more were John 15:5, 7–8. She recited the words that Jesus declared, "I am the vine, you are the branches; he who abides in Me, and I in him, he bears much fruit; for without Me you can do nothing…. If you abide in Me, and My words abide in you, you will ask what you desire, and it shall be done for you. By this My Father is glorified, that you bear much fruit, so you will be My disciples." She realized she was being taught how to abide in her soul; patiently, courageously, all day, continually, and eagerly so she would bear much fruit in His name and for His honor and glory.

At the end of her search, JC reflected on what she had gathered from her assignment. The last point stated was the one that linked both assignments together. She was given the task to read Exodus 24:12–18 and Exodus 34:29. She realized she would see the waiting process, fruit borne, and the glory of the Lord. What was revealed was the importance of waiting on and for the Father. He showed through His Word how Moses and other servants of old waited for Him. Moses taught the concept to the elders of Israel who, in turn, were to teach it to the people. Moses waited six days in one spot until the Father called him on the seventh day to enter into the cloud to commune with Him. Then He spent forty days and nights in the presence of the Lord. Joshua and the elders were obedient to the command of Moses to wait until He returned from the presence of God. Therefore, it took Moses six days of waiting before the Lord called him to the top of the mountain and then he spent forty days with the Father. Therefore, the people waited approximately forty-six days for Moses and the elders to return to them.

When Moses returned from being with the Lord, Aaron and all the Israelites saw his face was radiant. JC grasped the concept the Father wants His children to wait in every area of their lives so His presence will shine in and through them for His greater glory. Each time one enters into His presence and waits on and for Him, He does what He desires in lives with great anticipation of moving one from glory to glory.

Thinking of her destiny and the promises made, she realized God had a purpose and plan. Until she was molded and traveled through the next stage of her journey, there was no way she could see how her destiny was to unfold with a focus on the souls of mankind. Her purpose was to fellowship through worship with the Father through the waiting process as He led her on the path to souls being saved for His kingdom. Her professional position was just an avenue used to open the door for the Father to work wonders.

JC had learned one more life lesson on the road to fulfilling her destiny—patience which was draped in the idea of abiding in Christ Jesus. Thus the transition of moving from glory to glory was sealed in JC's mind that morning—another lesson learned!

MOVING LEVELS—
GLORY TO GLORY

The thought of moving levels in and before God was something entirely new to JC. She had never heard of such a thing, nor could she fathom the idea it was something God was doing to her for His glory. In order to understand the context of what the Father was sharing with her, she chose to ask for a clear and concise meaning. JC wanted to know what was the Father's glory, what it looked like, and what it meant that she was being moved from glory to glory?

In her mind, she felt at some point there must be information in a journal that would help her understand some essence of the Father's glory. She searched through the tapes that remained untouched, but all efforts were futile. The next place to start, of course, would be her Bible dictionary. JC grabbed a new journal and pen and began her search to gain clarity of the word *glory* and its significance to God. JC knew worship would create an atmosphere for God to visit with her, so she immediately entered into a time of praise and thanksgiving, all the while remembering it was important to wait patiently for God to share His thoughts with her.

In the stillness of her worship, God spoke,

> I am moving you from glory to glory, and I have placed
> My glory over you. Little do you realize, you have seen

My glory—for all people have seen it. What I desire is for you to search for understanding of My glory. In all you do, know I am My glory and I sent My glory to you and all mankind in the form of My Son, Jesus Christ.

In the silence that followed, JC begin to ask herself, when had she seen the glory of God and how did He manifest Himself to her? Basically, what did it look like? She began to pray that the Holy Spirit would bring to mind instances where she had seen the glory of God. She wrote her thoughts and then she read them aloud as if to say, "Is this what You are talking about, Lord?"

Lord, I remember when I was eighteen years old one of my uncles was sick in the hospital. As I sat outside in the lobby, I remember looking toward his room and seeing a deep golden cast emerge from his room and within seconds it disappeared. Lord, when I went to ask my mother what was going on, she told me my uncle had just died and gone home to be with You. Lord, the second thought that has come to mind is some thirty years later. I remember praying for a lady across the street who had been sick and needed a healing from You. As I followed Your command to pray for her (for many were praying for her), I looked across the street to her house, I saw a golden cast above her house. Days later, the report came back she had no trace of cancer in her body. The third time I remember seeing a golden cast was when I was in a meeting and You had warned me not to participate in the lewd behavior and conversation that surfaced among the people. At that moment, I remember looking up in front of me and seeing a golden cast in the room. Such warmth emerged as I smiled and realized You meant You would be with me wherever I go. Lord, I understand Your glory is seen in creation, but what does it mean in the context of what You say You are doing with me? I guess I shall move forward with the command given to search for understanding.

With the command to search for understanding before her, JC decided to think of her journey and all she had encountered. As she reflected upon her experiences, she decided to ask questions that would guide her. She voiced immediately, "It is important for me to know how the Father revealed His glory—in what form, to whom, and under what circumstances. Hopefully, I can draw conclusions as to what God means as He is moving me from glory to glory." Before JC could research an answer to her questions, she had to know what the word *glory* meant. She began to read aloud: "The word *glory* means radiance, brilliance, splendor, honor, beauty and greatness." Then she turned her attention to how the Father revealed His glory—the form seen by man. As she scanned through her Bible concordance, she found the glory of the Lord appeared in a cloud by day and a pillar of fire by night. The glory also appeared as a consuming fire on top of the mountain, in the heavens, fire coming down from heaven, and in the face of Jesus Christ. JC realized she could not list every revelation of the glory of God, but she knew God is limitless in His ability to reveal Himself. She read and surmised that God had revealed Himself to people. She named a few that she read about such as the children of Israel, Moses, Isaiah, Solomon, Stephen, Deborah, the shepherds, Magi, Ezekiel, Paul, Anna, Peter, and John. She also noted the Scriptures indicated His glory would be revealed to everyone (Revelation 1:7; Isaiah 40:5).

A further search revealed descriptors that accompany the word *glory* which were linked to the reality of God and His attributes as a way to commensurate the authenticity of His name and nature. The examples she found were Psalm 29:2 which states, "Give unto the Lord the glory due to His name; worship the Lord in the beauty of holiness," and "blessed be His glorious name forever; and let the whole earth be filled with His glory" (Psalm 72:19). JC saw the descriptors alluded to Him. The examples she read were:

- glory and dominion (1 Peter 4:11);
- glory and honor (Revelation 21:26);
- glory and greatness (Deuteronomy 5:24);
- greatness, power, glory, victory, and majesty (1 Chronicles 29:11);
- shield and glory (Psalm 3:3);
- glory, mercy and truth (Psalm 115:1); and
- glory, majesty, dominion, and power (Jude 1:25).

She began to see how God had revealed His glory through the heavens, earth, fire, a cloud, the face of Jesus Christ, and to everyone on earth. She knew it was important to know when and under what conditions the Father showed Himself to people. Her search was focused on the presence of God—His glory among the people. She wrote a few of the examples as she mediated on what was occurring during those times.

- experiencing the burning bush (Exodus 3:2);
- delivering the children from Egypt (Exodus 7–11);
- parting of the Red Sea (Exodus 14:13–31);
- complaining against God (Exodus 16:8–10);
- speaking with God (Exodus 34:29–35);

- erecting the tabernacle (Exodus 40:34–38);
- gathering of nations and tongues (Isaiah 66:18);
- worshipping (2 Chronicles 7:1);
- suffering, trials, tribulations (1 Peter 4:12; 2 Corinthians 4:17;);
- revealing Jesus Christ through His birth, death, and resurrection (Luke 2; Matthew 27–28); and
- exalting of Jesus Christ (Psalm 21:5; Isaiah 6:3; Hebrews 1:3, Hebrews 9:5; Matthew 16:27; Mark 13:26 and Revelation 1:7).

JC stopped to gather herself. As she began to review she said,

Father, I see only a glimpse of what You want to share with me. As I read Your Word, I see each event or encounter encompasses a level of intimacy with You as You seek to bring each person who is called by Your name and whom You have created for Your glory (Isaiah 43:7) into Your bosom for Your own great pleasure. As You draw me closer to You, You shower me with Your love. I see the linkage to the word *glory* that brings forth the awesomeness of who You are! As You move me from glory to glory, I am aware You are preparing me to be ready when Christ is revealed at His second coming. You are refining people as pure gold by Your divine power and knowledge because You have called people to You by glory and virtue (2 Peter 1:3). Father, I sense a small part of the concept of growth and understanding as You move me from level to level in order to fill me with Your presence. I have gained understanding as I move from test to test that You are moving me from glory to glory because the passing of each test reveals more of You to me and in me. Now, I get it—I recognize that "tribulation produces perseverance; and perseverance, character; and character, hope; and hope does not disappoint, because the love of God has been poured out in our hearts through the Holy Spirit who was given to us" (Romans 5:3–5).

This entire wilderness experience has been about the Father teaching me about Himself; His love, hope, and destiny. Learning to get through the journey God's way, the first time around, is significant to learning who the Father is. Surviving the journey is found in one's ability to humble him/herself through worshipping and praising the God of the universe. As I encounter the holiness of God, I find great pleasure in knowing His purpose leads to my destiny before Him. I have comprehended the value of abiding in Him as He guides me to the destiny He created for me before the foundation of the world. In His timing, I will grow more in love with Him because He has created this relationship for His great pleasure as He covers me in His canopy of love—His glory.

JC whispered a love song to the Father as she sensed Him being pleased with her insight about His glory. As she closed her journal and placed her pen on the table, she promised herself to always value the intimate times with the Father and to cherish the highs and lows of life, for in each situation God was drawing her closer to Himself, into the place of His abiding love.

STEP FIVE

Step into your destiny with a clear understanding of your purpose!

Jesus stated, "For I have come down from heaven, not to do My own will, but the will of Him who sent Me (John 6:38). The key learning is to align yourself with Jesus Christ and walk out His purpose for your life. It begins with you accepting Jesus as Lord and Savior and then gaining clarity of your purpose. Just remember, sometimes in destiny there's a setback before a comeback. Even in the midst of what might not look like destiny or feel like purpose, God is with you.

Take a few minutes to reflect over these three sections to stimulate your thinking.

Word Study: destiny, purpose, wait, glory

1. _____ is the predetermined course of events which is beyond human control.
2. Great honor, praise, renown, adoration, majestic beauty, and splendor is _____.
3. To remain or rest in expectation or to tarry in readiness is to _____.
4. The object toward which one strives or an aim or goal is _____.

Questions:

1. What do you see as your purpose for living?
2. What evidence do you have that you are following God's destiny for your life?
3. When you face obstacles, what strategies do you use to get back on the path?

Tips:

1. Write three affirmations to support your purpose. Read them daily and act upon them.
2. Look for ways to improve your skills as you move toward your destiny.
3. Remove things from your life that are impeding your life.

SECTION 6

From the Wilderness to the Promised Land

Have you ever been to an event with a friend and realized people in the room did not know your friend and it became your responsibility to introduce your friend to everyone? Have you ever noticed when introductions are made, people introduce a person by position or status while sharing little to no information about the person? JC knew she had been guilty of this very thing—introducing people while occasionally missing the most important quality of the person.

As she thought to herself about her journey, she knew she had experienced a great love affair with God but at some point had failed to introduce Him by what she considered His most important attribute, "I AM."

In the midst of all things, she was quite aware "I AM" had traveled second by second, minute by minute, hour by hour, and day by day with her. She had experienced in the wilderness journey that the way had been paved and doors opened to sustain her as she went from a spiritual journey that began to be revealed in her earthly walk.

Thus, JC asked herself, "Who is Jesus?" She succumbed to the thought that simply introducing Him as King of Kings and Lord of Lords was not allowing her to know the intimate One called Savior of the world. She wanted to know the One who is the Son of God and who has the distinct, awesome privilege to sit at the Father's right hand.

JC knew every good search began with knowing the person's name and its meaning (origin), thus her search unfolded as she opened a journal and positioned a set of tapes marked, "Names and Titles of Jesus."

LEARNING JESUS IN
LIFE'S JOURNEY

The moment JC sat down to review her journal and listen to a set of tapes, she knew she was about to be reminded of a place in time that reshaped her life because it was a time that caused her to see Jesus Christ as the multifaceted, multi-dimensional God who declared in her walk He was "I AM." True to her thought, as she turned the pages of her journal and read silently, she found a revelation of Jesus as "I AM." She had written a statement she believed Jesus Himself had given to her. The statement written was—"I am He! I am the One who is present and active in the day-to-day operations of your life; praying for you, directing the battle over you, and ministering to you." JC had circled the last line of the statement which read, "I am one with the Father—I am in the Father and the Father is in Me."

JC chose to listen to a tape because it had been sometime since she had heard events to describe what had transpired in her life over a period of time. She pushed play and heard words that introduced her to Jesus all over again. She smiled as she scribbled the words heard, words that lifted her soul to a higher level.

> Simply stated, Your name is Jesus! Jesus, if I am ever going to introduce You to someone, it would help if You introduced Yourself to me. I know in this journey

You have been with me, but can You share a little more about Yourself in the journey. According to my Bible dictionary, Your name is derived from the Hebrew word, "Joshua" (Y'shua or Yeshua) or "Je-Hoshua," meaning Jehovah is salvation. Christ is equivalent to the Hebrew word, "Messiah (Meshiach), the Anointed One." I also see Your name—Jesus Christ—is "I am," Yahweh, rendered as Lord (Father, Son, and Holy Spirit), which is derived from the verb, *hayah*, to be. Now, the verb "to be" is the state of being, always in existence; to equal in meaning or identity or to exist in a specified place. The reference to You as I AM reveals You have existed from the beginning of the creation of the world. Genesis 1:1 indicates Your origin is from antiquity. In Micah 5:2, it states Your goings forth are from old, from everlasting. And Hebrews 13:8 declares that You are the same yesterday, today, and forever.

I know the Bible teaches You are the Word that became flesh and my source of strength. The Father has always referred to You as His Son, my Savior and Lord, the One who provides for me. I feel Your presence in my daily walk as I read Your Word. You manifest Yourself in the way that brings life to every circumstance I face. I appreciate You revealing Yourself as my sovereign Lord who is my bread, light, door, shepherd, resurrection, truth, and vine. The reality of the connection to You through those words is causing me to understand You as my spiritual food, guide, restoration, assurance, and rest.

As the tape continued, JC looked at the beginning and ending dates of the journal. Two months were given to this research with the last several pages given to a list marked with Scripture references to Jesus as "I am." JC picked up her Bible and began to read each Scripture marked with a reference to Jesus as "I am." Those read were:

- I AM who I AM (Exodus 3:14)
- I am He. I am the First. I am also the last;(Isaiah 48:12) the Alpha and Omega (Revelation 1:8)
- I, the Lord am holy (Leviticus 20:26)
- Be holy, for I am holy (1 Peter 1:16)
- I, even I, am He, and there is no God besides Me (Deuteronomy 32:39)
- Before Abraham was born, I AM (John 8:58)
- I am He (John 18:5)
- I am the bread of life (John 6:35)
- I am the light of the world (John 8:12)
- I am the door of the sheep (John 10:7)
- I am the good shepherd (John 10:11)
- I am the resurrection and the life (John 11:25)
- I am the way, and the truth and the life (John 14:6)
- I am the true vine (John 15:1)

Rereading those Scriptures at this point in time allowed JC to reflect. She knew the initial stages of her journey were filled with questions about the events happening in her daily walk, but as she read the contents of her journal, she saw where Jesus had been revealed more and more, which caused her to begin to understand the ultimate relationship that had grown out of her cry for answers and His ability to draw her to His Word, really served as her daily bread, strength, sustaining power, and deliverance. She could now see how Jesus maintained the truth of

His Word by being her sustainer and deliverer as well as her brother, healer, priest, Lord of breakthrough, and faithful and true witness. She could literally see where Jesus had walked with her on this journey of tests, trials, and tribulations and how His presence became the stability needed to carry her to victory. In the revelation of Jesus as "I AM," JC could see the Scriptures more clearly as the discovery of Jesus' position, order, and place emerged from the context of the Bible. As she continued to review notes, a bright light—a moment of expressible joy—filled her. She finally grasped the information written about Jesus. While she knew it was only the surface of who He is, she chose to read the information and record it so if she lost her notes, she would have the recording. She found a blank tape and began to record old information that sparked a bright light. She spoke the words clearly,

> In researching the *position* of Christ, two categories emerged: the first is compiled of His ownership, description, and title followed by His status, order, rank and, place in heaven as well as on earth. His ownership, description, and title define His authority. This is revealed through His name as the Son of God, incarnate God, infinite One, shadow of the Almighty, and zealous Zion's righteous king. Jesus is the Ancient of Days who laid the foundation of the earth with the heavens being the works of His hands. He is author of life and heir of all things. He is the lion of Judah as well as the victorious, mighty warrior and captain of the Lord's hosts, who is superior in all things. He is the anchor and guardian of souls. He declares, "Behold, all souls are Mine; as the soul of the father, as well as the soul of the son is Mine" (Ezekiel 18:4) for they have

been bought with a price (1Corinthians 6:20) that could only come through the shedding of blood by the Lamb of God, our Passover Lamb (1 Corinthians 5:7) and our Redeemer (Isaiah 43:14; Psalm 34:22).

The throne is His forever and ever and the righteous scepter is the scepter of His kingdom. The earth is His and all it contains, the world and those who dwell in it. He has founded it upon the seas and established it upon the rivers. He declares, "The silver is Mine, and the gold is Mine (Haggai 2:8). Every beast of the forest is Mine, and the cattle on a thousand hills. I know all the birds of the mountains; and the wild beasts of the field are Mine" (Psalm 50:10–11). He is majesty on high, Lord God, the Almighty, potentate (ruler) over the kings of the earth (Revelation 1:5).

Since all things have been given to Jesus, a picture of His *status*—eminence, distinction, prominence, and notoriety—was revealed. I see throughout my journey, His distinction was seen in His position as the Son of God, Son of Man, the Word, Immanuel, advocate, author and finisher of faith, teacher, shepherd, and intercessor. Each revelation strengthened my understanding of His importance: His worthiness, holiness, righteousness, purity, and majesty. As events unfolded during this journey, Jesus unveiled and released His power, coupled with the assurance He alone is the indescribable, free gift given to aid me.

I see the *order* of Christ proclaimed through His ability to declare His instruction in all events. He is revealed as the Alpha and Omega, the first and the last, and the beginning and ending of all things. As the forerunner, the prototype and original example of all creation, He demonstrated His position as the first fruits; the One who became the firstborn from the dead; the resurrection and the life. His actions of love were demonstrated as He was marred and pierced and eventually hung on the cross. He resumed His position as my first love, a position that taught me about loving Him with my whole heart. The position of being my first love brought such joy and peace because the One who loves me wanted nothing more than the opportunity to declare His banner of love over me.

The *rank* held by the Lord is revealed in Isaiah 55:4—leader and commander over every nation and the ruler over all the kingdoms of the earth. He is the chief cornerstone and chief shepherd. Without the cornerstone, the building will collapse and be ruined. The Bible reveals no greater foundation can be laid than Jesus Christ. I need to remember to build only upon His foundation. As the chief shepherd, He guides me in and through the wilderness experience with His rod and staff, so learning will be useful and growth can be seen. I understand that with His rod, He will correct me and with His staff, He will guide my every turn.

The last position researched is *place*. I have read that His kingdom lies in the recesses of the north, promotion comes from the north and new beginnings come from the east. Genesis 3:24 describes how man was driven out of the garden and at the east of the garden of Eden, the Lord stationed the cherubim with a flaming sword which turned every direction, to guard the way to the tree of life. I see the sword turns north and south, east and west, and forms a cross which helps me understand Jesus is the way to the tree of life. In everything I do, I must remember He has been everywhere and is everywhere for He alone knows my past, present, and future, thus He knows my life's calling!

JC stopped the recorder and reflected over the knowledge gained from studying Jesus' name. She was amazed at the amount of information she had collected over the two-month time period and how much she had seen of the very nature of Jesus through His name, titles, and descriptions. She recognized that through the journey she had seen Jesus as a stable rock—One who was strong, dependable, firm, and immovable. All she had to do was rest in His arms. JC could see the growth made as she had trusted Jesus with her heart, mind, body, and soul. She knew as she reviewed her notes, a great relationship had emerged as she found herself more freely able to introduce Jesus to people with more knowledge of His role and quality of life. Her lifelong dream was to tell people about the stabilizer of her life, her friend and companion, Jesus Christ—sovereign Lord of the universe—the One who declared she was ready to enter into her Promised Land for He had made her ready!

BEING PREPARED TO ENTER YOUR PROMISED LAND

JC could see through her journals that she was leaving the wilderness and preparing to enter into her Promised Land. She knew much had transpired because of the growth made by the direct intervention of the Father. So she took a few minutes to reflect over the path. She knew from a study on spiritual gifts that her primary gift was teaching. She also knew she enjoyed organizing things and leading groups of people to develop the best skills they could to assist others, namely through education. With that knowledge, she began to search the Scriptures to see how God used people to bring about His plan for their lives. The reading of Ephesians 4:11–12, which mentioned the five ministry or primary gifts—apostles, prophets, evangelists, pastors, and teachers— aligned itself to Romans 12:6–8, which revealed prophecy, ministry/ service, teaching, exhortation, giving, administration/leading, and mercy as motivational gifts given by the Spirit of God. She chose to look at the lives of two of her favorite Bible characters, Moses and David with Joshua following close behind. Her thoughts of course, had to be written or recorded because it was her style for remembering. She began to record her thoughts.

As a young child, Moses lived and learned the life of a prince. His calling appears to be a mission based on learning how to rule (administer) over a people. When I think of a prince, I think of the daily commitments that involve lots of meetings or engagements. His day-to-day events must have been filled with meetings, engagements, and activities that prepared him to one day lead Egypt. Now, when Moses fled from the presence of Pharaoh, he found himself in the presence of the daughters of the priest of Midian. What I remember is Moses stood up and helped the daughters of the Midianite priest and watered their flock. He delivered the daughters of the priest from the hand of their enemies and cared for their flock. Later in his walk, Moses used his day-to-day learning to lead and serve the people of God. Through the insight and wisdom of his father-in-law, Jethro, the Midianite priest, he learned a greater depth of organizational skills to help him shepherd the people of God.

David's calling was to shepherd. It was during his time in the field caring for his sheep he learned organizational skills and combat strategies. Later in life, David became the most beloved king who had demonstrated his ability to be a valiant warrior. His love for the Lord and ministering to the people of Israel allowed for his talents to be seen by man and orchestrated before God.

Both Moses and David had a priestly or kingly life that assisted them throughout their journey upon this earth. They were called to feed the sheep, thus, minister to the people of God. Moses and David travelled through a wilderness experience as they were prepared to move into their Promised Land, one that focused on teaching and leading the people of God and learning to follow God's heart. In all these men did, their number one use of their gifts was to serve the Lord and spend quality time before and with God.

> As I think about the preparation process, it is vitally important I remember I have One instructor who is God. He is the One with the outline or blueprint before Him, and He is the One who knows where the obstacles are as well as where and when the victories will emerge. I now see God had to prepare me spiritually to take the land first before I could take it in the physical realm.

JC felt a great peace sweep over her because she could sense the desire of God the Father to make her into a treasured possession that would continue to bring Him glory. She truly understood her walk through the wilderness journey was one that had to occur and it would bring great dividends because of the way she had experience His faithfulness in all things. She wrote,

> There are five key points learned in and through the journey and preparation process: (1) trust in God, (2) depend on Him, (3) develop faith, (4) learn to engage in spiritual warfare His way, and (5) walk in total obedience, all the time expressing love and appreciation to God. It is important to capture, cultivate, multiply, and harvest the land God gives so souls may be won as God receives the glory.

> I want to remember to wait and enter the Promised Land on the Father's timetable. It is important to wait because the territory is taken only when the principalities and

powers over the territory are destroyed by God's heavenly warriors. My role is to pray, fast, and be obedient to the voice of God and to be ready to enter into the land as His child, His chosen vessel to bring Him glory, not by the title or position of the job.

What the Father has taught me is this; many people may think they are walking in their Promised Land, but they are not. They don't address things from a spiritual stance therefore they miss their harvest before the Father. But those who are walking in their Promised Land are yielding great gains for the kingdom.

I need to read about Joshua, because he was the one who studied under Moses and was appointed by God to lead the people into the Promised Land. What I remember is Joshua was the son of Nun and a member of the tribe of Ephraim, the tribe that later formed the heart of the northern kingdom of Israel. He was one of two men who brought back a positive report after spying out the Promised Land because he believed what God had said. He was a military leader as well as a spiritual leader for the nation of Israel. Joshua was commissioned by God who gave specific words about what he needed to do as Israel's new leader. As I read Joshua 1:3 and verses 5-9, I see Joshua was told:

- "Every place that the sole of your foot will tread, I have given you, as I said to Moses."

- "No man shall be able to stand before you all the days of your life; as I was with Moses, so I will be with you; I will not leave your nor forsake you."
- "Be strong and of good courage for to this people you shall divide as an inheritance the land which I swore to their fathers to give them."
- "Only be strong and very courageous; that you may observe to do according to all the law which Moses My servant commanded you; do not turn from it to the right hand or to the left, that you may prosper wherever you go."
- "This Book of the Law shall not depart from your mouth, but you shall meditate in it day and night, that you may observe to do according to all that is written in it. For then you will make your way prosperous, and then you will have good success."
- "Be strong and of good courage; do not be afraid, nor be dismayed, for the LORD, your God is with you wherever you go."

As I examine the words God commanded the people to do before they entered the Promised Land, I do see how God worked and He prepared me to enter into my Promised Land. The same four things He said to Joshua are the very things His Word reveals for all people. The four things He told Joshua to have the people do, are (1) prepare provisions because they would enter the land in three days, (2) consecrate themselves, for the Lord was going to do wonders among them, (3) make flint knives and circumcise again the sons of Israel the second time, and (4) celebrate the Passover at Gilgal, which was the first place of worship for the Israelites under Joshua's leadership.

The four things every child of God must do before they can enter their Promised Land is (1) prepare to enter in, (2) consecrate themselves before the Lord, (3) circumcise their hearts, and (4) celebrate the victory won in the heavenly realm.

JC stopped the tape to focus on the big picture. Now she could see every little detail of events held a special purpose. In the early aspects of the wilderness experience when the pain was great and the struggles almost unbearable, she realized God had been teaching her about His love, mission, and how her obedience moved her into a place where God the Father could trust her with His work. She wrote what came to mind. God has:

- given the vision, mission, and the name of the land he wants conquered;
- given directions to follow pertaining to the land;
- placed my life in a wilderness experience so things would be purged from my life to prepare me for the Promised Land;
- planted my feet in what I called Midian (a holding place for however long it takes). Midian was the place God sent Moses to show Him how to defeat the enemy, defend the people, and feed them;
- anointed me for seven days. He used one of His servants to carry out His task.
- commanded me to consecrate myself unto Him through a fast; and
- declared me promoted in the heavenly realm while I was waiting for the open door so I could walk into the Promised Land He stated was mine.

When she could think of nothing else, she felt a strong tug on her heart, one she knew was an awe-inspiring touch that caused her to humble herself before the One she loved so dearly. As she moved to the floor, she heard herself thanking Jesus for introducing Himself to her at a greater degree and for being the revelation of her solid rock. She thanked Him for being a stable place to rest from the heat (fire) of life, as well as being her foundation of support and source of strength. As she prayed, she thanked Jesus for being her foundational stone, a precious, white, pure stone that held her in the wilderness journey and now was ready to lead her into her Promised Land. She called out to Him and began to sing words.

"You are my Rock and fortress, a rock of habitation and I will commune with You on a daily basis. You are my stronghold and my Rock of refuge who saved me from the troubles that plagued my soul. You are my Rock of the wilderness, my Rock, my Rock, my Rock!"

As she lay on the floor, humbled by God's presence, she sensed Him saying, "JC, your life is not determined by material things, but by the growth made in your walk before Me. All I have desired and so desire from man is an intimate relationship with him. I have showered you in my love and will continue to develop our love affair because it is about the souls! My Son, your Rock, will always be your guide and My Spirit will always be your covering for I have given them to aid you in your walk before Me. As you enter your Promised Land, know all things have been crafted by Me to bring Me glory. I will not fail you nor forsake you for I truly love you with all of My heart, mind, and soul! Enter your Promised Land and lean on the Rock of your salvation, My Son, Jesus!"

STEP SIX

Develop your identity in Christ!

To introduce Jesus by one of His greatest qualities brings wholeness to life. Psalm 31:3 states two qualities of Christ that can support any transition of one's life. Memorize these words: "For You are my rock and my fortress; therefore, for Your name's sake lead and guide me." So the key to learning your identity is to know the One in whom you trust each moment of your life.

Take a few minutes to reflect over these three sections to stimulate your thinking.

Word Study: Jesus, position, status, order, place

1. _____ is the Savior of the world.
2. The ownership or description of one's authority is _____.
3. To classify or categorize is the meaning of _____.
4. _____ is the location, space, or area of something.
5. The prominence, distinction, or notoriety of a person is known as _____.

Questions:

1. When was the last time you searched for Jesus upon the pages of the Bible? Begin a list of every name or title you find.

2. What is your relationship with Jesus? How do you see Him? Friend, lover of you soul, etc.

Tips:

1. Each day for thirty days, practice the presence of God by calling on Jesus by His name or title throughout the day. Examples: Lord, Savior, Atonement, Deliverer, Sustainer, Rock, etc.

2. Write a prayer to the Lord, and then pray and meditate on the Word of God.

SECTION 7

CONCLUSION

"All good things must come to an end." It's an expression many people say but sometimes really don't understand what truly comes to an end or if there really is an end to something. Instead of saying those words, JC reflected over the words she'd scribbled on a sheet of paper. As she gazed at her words, she saw "love and improvement" etched in charcoaled color as if she had dug the words deeply into the paper. She laughed because she could see her journey portrayed more about *love* and *improvement*, which equaled growth, than the harshness of pain and suffering. She chose in no way to downplay the experiences but realized in any journey, the entire process had a message—the message or the reality of the message would culminate in the final version of the experiences she had come to know as her life.

JC turned the paper over to see what she had written on the back. To her amazement, she saw "Sunday, 1:30 a.m. *Go tell it on the mountain,*" followed by the words, "interventions and experiences." She sat still as her mind rehearsed the day and time plus those words. She knew it meant something, but what was the message that lingered within those words? What she chose to do was at the heart of what emerged from the very first time she entered into her little prayer closet. She chose to search for meaning in the confinement of her tapes, journals, and heart. JC felt as though she lived her life through a mirror because of how God had intervened and caused her to grow each step of the way.

JC knew the recalculation of events of those past years had shaped her into a woman who now relied on God for everything—His intervention in every experience she faced. She wondered why she had written the words, *Go tell it on the mountain,* and connected them to interventions and experiences. The only thing she could do was search for an answer and being JC, she did just that!

INTERVENTIONS AND EXPERIENCES

JC rose early in the morning to finish her work as she prepared to completely clean out the little prayer closet and organize her final belongings into the new room created to house her multiple books, videos, CDs, and cassettes. She wanted so much to listen to the final stack of tapes but knew she had to have everything in place so she could finish her Bible course for the semester. She had grown so much in the church's school of ministry that she became involved in the mission trips where she taught Bible courses as well as preached sermons. In her mind, she only taught the Word of God, but her mentor had declared that she preached and did it well.

JC worked for several hours. She knew once she sat down, she would be finished for the day. So to keep her focused on moving, she decided to date her materials and place them on the shelf. The thought of listening to one more tape surfaced, but JC became preoccupied with the thought lurking in her mind about the words written on that sheet of paper. She wondered why she had written down the day, time, and words on the back side of the paper. By now, she knew not having an answer was not a good thing for her. JC appreciated the fact that big ideas or little details meant something to her. After all, that's how God had trained her to respect the gift of knowledge and wisdom found deep within her soul.

So as the day progressed, JC found herself setting up the tape recorder to listen to it as she continued to unpack boxes and place materials on the bookshelf. The time of reflection would be a great way to keep her alert and moving so her chore could be completed before she turned in for the evening.

JC began to listen to the final tapes found on the table. JC chuckled as she heard herself describe how she'd pulled the Bible dictionary off the shelf to define the word *intervention,* and how she'd talked to herself about what an intervention was and why such a small word was so important. What appeared to be an odd conversation caused JC to rewind the tape and start it again. In the midst of the replay, she heard herself describing an educational process used in school. It was the ILP or IIP process used with a student who was on an individual learning plan (ILP) or an individual intervention plan (IIP). In this process, a team of teachers are assigned a number of students, and they convene to design a plan for each student within their cohort or cluster. The purpose of the plan is to make each individual child successful in school. The team of teachers focuses on the child's strengths, limitations, and needs. The teachers discuss the child, goals are written, timelines are set, and safety nets (strategies) are infused into the plan with a monitoring process and review dates established.

JC asked herself why she would put this type of information on a tape and in such detail. She continued to listen for some clue as to the purpose of the tape. She heard about the lead teacher assuming responsibility to meet with the student while articulating with great anticipation that success will occur, how the team is able to revisit the plan if little or no success is made toward a specific goal, how the process continues until success is demonstrated in every area of that child's learning, and finally how mini celebrations occur as a gauge to encourage continual movement toward the goals identified.

She even listened to her explanation that an intervention was an act or process of continual involvement by God; that it was His concentrated attentiveness to the details of a designed plan created by Him for one's life. She even heard herself say the intervention was God's responsibility: He was obligated to provide strategies and resources to aid persons in their growth process and the intervention is a limitless one. The description that followed included a breakdown of how God convenes with Jesus and His Holy Spirit who understand and are able to appreciate the ultimate goal of restoring the spiritual relationship He desired with man. The final statement caused JC to gasp, as she heard that God always performs His acts of love through supernatural interventions as He implements His individual plan for each person.

At that point, the light bulb came on. JC stopped the tape. She grasped the information revealed how God had intervened through events so she could determine the successes based on His interventions.

JC knew the evening was drawing to a close and night would be upon her, but she chose to stop and pull out a pen and pad in an attempt to recapture the areas of her life, thinking about which ones had to be addressed and revisited based on the contents of the tape. She knew some lessons had to be learned twice. Even with re-teaching occurring, JC knew success had occurred and was occurring. As usual, JC chose to write her thoughts, and being a determined person, knew she would read them aloud so she could hear herself. She titled her little paper with a question. She wrote, "How has God intervened in my walk?"

The revelation of God's intervention is seen through Him *demonstrating* His love for me, *teaching* the importance of improving my relationship with Him as a source of growth, *obeying* His Word, *molding* me to love others, and *giving* me a greater vision to display

147

His involvement in the affairs of man. I can remember throughout my journey, God shared so much about His love. He showered me with kindness, patience, and gentleness, which reflected Him as the source of giving. As I read 1 Corinthians 13 in an attempt to grasp the meaning of love, He shared the meaning of the word love as *doing*. He wanted me to understand He is constantly in motion for His people. These words were always a part of our conversation—acting, saving, rescuing, delivering, disciplining, celebrating, and enjoying. The Father emphasized love is not a feeling like I think it is, but it is His selflessness toward people. He reminded me on more than one occasion that people think they have to do something to earn His love instead of just giving themselves to Him, which is His desire. It has helped me to remember if we would become an unselfish people, truly self-sacrificing, we would exhibit the love of the Father and demonstrate that love to our fellow man.

I perceive the key to Him demonstrating His love was revealed in His ability to work out the details while convincingly supporting me in every challenge. It was the "doing" that captured my heart so improvements could be charted as a record of growth. Even in the midst of my mistakes, His love never ceased. He gently, and occasionally sternly, guided me back onto the path so I could continue to make growth toward His goals. He reaffirmed His unfailing love by bringing promises to pass. He lavished me in His love by drawing me into His presence as His sweet, tender hands encompassed me.

As I begin to think about the areas of growth, I find faith, patience, and praying are three areas that reveal a great degree of improvement. I noticed throughout the many journal entries and tapes God continued to tell me to trust Him. From those conversations emerged the words *relentless* and *combative*. He told me while listening to one of His generals preach a sermon at church that the faith she demonstrated as she preached His word was the kind of faith I needed to have.

I began to understand from that point on, if God said something was going to happen or if He had done something in my behalf, the struggle to believe Him dissipated. I no longer struggled but waited patiently for Him to tell me when something would occur or wait for it to materialize. I noticed I became more patient with my family and events that occurred throughout the day. If I failed in a task or assignment, I sought forgiveness, got it, and moved forward instead of wallowing in self-pity or mental persecution. I no longer mentally or emotionally beat myself up over failures because I had became patient with myself and accepted the fact I wasn't choosing to be disobedient, but it was human frailty at its finest point. I also knew I had an advocate who knew and loved me in spite of myself.

During my prayer time, an increased presence of the Lord hovered over me. The Father had indicated I should increase my prayer time. The point is, the trust I learned by relying upon His Spirit to intercede with groans beyond my comprehension helped me rest in the security that Jesus, the great Intercessor, was always on the job in my behalf.

Those acts of obedience brought such joy. Obeying God became an avenue for our continual conversations to occur. The Father had indicated listening to His voice and obeying His commandments brought blessings upon a person. I believed I had lived through all of the curses by disobeying the Lord because I didn't heed His voice. Now, my desire and goal are to obey because I prefer to live victoriously and receive a hundredfold blessing instead of settling no blessing at all. The total blessing from the Father could only come through obedience. The act of obedience was confirming my love to and for the Father. Through obedience He was teaching me love. The Father wanted me to move beyond liking all people to loving my fellow man. He knew I truly liked people and wanted none to perish, but it was going to take His love and me being molded into His image for the love of the Lord to emerge from my life.

There are three important revelations pertaining to love that emerged on this journey. He (1) communicated his love on a continual basis, (2) showed me His love throughout His Word, and (3) commanded I tell people of His love on a daily basis

There were times I would be in a public place and He would say, "Tell that person I love him/her." In the beginning, it was a struggle for me to open my mouth to tell a person God loved them or to say, God loves you, because I was concerned with what people thought about some stranger coming out of the blue with that statement. But as I experienced more of His love and heard Him say, "Thank you for being my hands and feet and allowing My love to flow through you," it became easier. Telling people God loved them ultimately became simpler when He put it in the perspective that sharing His love brought His vision for the world into a greater focus.

As I pondered over His words, I thought this vision for the world must be so complicated it requires monstrous implementation. But simply put, His vision is, "None should perish." He gave His vision through John 3:16 and He is implementing that vision as He continuously involves Himself in the affairs of man.

I remember searching for the meaning of *affairs* and when I found it, I was astounded that the first reference was the word *relationship*. The reference included dealings, contacts, interactions, and associations. The way I was picturing the "affairs of man," God was engaging in world events, but what He wanted me to see was the affairs of man meant His spiritual relationship, His dealings and interactions in the lives of people. He wanted me to understand He was on a campaign to alter the affairs of man through a loving, wooing encounter. He was addressing every aspect of a relationship by working through homes and churches that welcomed His Spirit, people giving of themselves, His anointed vessels going before kings or government leaders in His love, and people having a heart to listen to and for Him.

He showed me through so many people during my journey that He was teaching people of His love by drawing them into a realm of safety as they faced challenges in their lives. I even said to Him as I listened to a lady share about the events of her life, that there are so many people who have faced more than I could ever think. But He quickly reminded me it was what He was doing and had done in the wilderness experience that was going to be an event to cause people to see that He is real. I recall Him telling me He would help people understand what they had gone through and how to be drawn into a loving relationship with Him just by the encounters and experiences of their daily lives.

JC paused as she concluded her moment of reflection. She had a very good idea as to what, why, and how God had intervened, but the one thought of the significance of the "Sunday morning, 1:30 a.m.—*Go tell it on the mountain*" notation remained a puzzle. As she thought to herself, she recognized so much had transpired, it would be humanly impossible to capture every event or experience from her past. But the one thing that had always been a ray of hope was her ability to present her request to the Father and wait for the Holy Spirit to bring to mind her heart's desire—and this time her heart longed to know the importance of that notation. As JC prayed for God to enlighten her mind and heart, she slowly recalled that all of the incidents, encounters, or happenings were experiences. The three experiences that changed her forever were hearing His Voice, experiencing His love, and enjoying His fellowship.

One mighty lesson emerged through her experiences, even during the initial struggle to accept that God was speaking to her. She had sought His voice and had learned God longs to speak to us, but people are too busy and allow too many distractions to interfere with hearing Him. JC surmised that somehow people allowed self or the enemy to come in and create a distraction, and so they lose the ability to hear. But she knew if people would begin to seek and trust Him, they would hear. She knew when He initially spoke, she didn't trust what she was hearing, but she'd continued to record the information. When God spoke, His voice was clear, concise, and literally consumed her mind (thoughts). She would hear "I am He," or hear her name called. The Father told her the very thoughts she had as He declared He was not Satan attempting to disguise himself as an angel of light. He did three things to assist her in knowing He was God:

- He introduced Himself as the Great God Jehovah and there is no other;
- He told her a secret desire she had since she was ten years old; and
- He showed in His Word how He spoke to the prophets of old and to David.

The Father helped her understand when He shared who He was that He is the One who sits on His throne. JC knew it was the Father because He stated the secret she had buried in her heart. He framed the secret in a question that caused her heart to melt. The next thing He did was to have her review how He was speaking to her when He wanted her to write what He was saying. She remembered the conversations began with these words, "Thus says the Lord or write My words." Then He took her throughout His Word to show her He had talked to His prophets throughout history in that fashion.

The final impact that solidified she was hearing His voice came while reading Psalm 50. JC was searching for the names of God. The chapter opened with Abhir (the mighty One), Elohim (the Lord) followed by Shaphat (judge) and El Elyon (most high). But as she reread the chapter, she wrote, "David is speaking in verses 1–6 and referring to Him or He," but in verses 7–15, she saw the words, "I will speak." At that point the Lord showed He was the One speaking and still speaks to His people today. JC knew He had answered a longing to hear His voice which led to experiencing His love.

JC began to think aloud. "The event which has been impressed in my spirit more than any event is the day I learned God only sees *red*. It happened at a conference where this lady who had faced some racial and ethnic comments shared that she had prayed and God told her He sees red! What an awesome God who only sees people through the blood of Jesus, His Son, which was shed for mankind. I have the wonderful privilege to travel upon the path of life each day experiencing His unconditional, uncomplicated, and unreserved love. All I had to do is invite Jesus into my heart. Coming to Jesus, uncovering all things, allowed Him to move in and set up residency in my heart. That one act of surrender and acceptance allowed Him the privilege of bringing me into a right, intimate relationship with Him. I realized I couldn't earn a relationship with Him or buy a relationship with Him, I just had to accept Him by faith and receive the true warmth and expression of love that could only come from the throne room of the Father!"

JC chuckled as she continued to expound on her experiences. Such joy filled her soul as she thought back to the day God had taught her about fellowship being friendship. For JC, it was the day she chose to keep her end of the relationship healthy. She remembered feeling ashamed before God because she had failed so many assignments. When she finally worked up enough nerve to go to Him, His focus was not on the failed assignments, but how she thought she couldn't come to Him after all He had shared and done. The words, "I am disappointed" rang in her ears that day. God was not disappointed in her but the fact that since they were friends and had come to trust each other that JC felt she couldn't come to Him just as she was. JC reflected on how she began to read her Bible and read a story as to how Israel had hurt the heart of God. She couldn't believe how the words practically jumped off the page as she continued to read. In her mind, she surely had not hurt the heart of God but, to her surprise as she continued to read, she saw where the Father was tenderhearted toward those who love Him. JC declared from that time on she would be sensitive to the heart of God since He was tender toward people especially when there was an established relationship He took time to pursue (woo), build, and maintain.

As JC stood and stretch her legs, she shook her head as she exclaimed, "You are truly an awesome God, One who waits for people to rise each day, so you can enter into fellowship with them. I can hardly grasp what it feels like to know that the Father in heaven waits for me to rise as He breathes His life into me for that day." As she sat back down, JC comprehended His interventions and experiences such as hearing His voice, experiencing His love, and fellowshipping with Him all derived from one source: His Son being poured out as love, mercy, goodness, and grace. She marveled at the opportunity to sit at His feet to know His heart's desire—that none should perish because He is love!

JC still waited to know more about that mysterious notation. She chose to sing the words to God as a message of love to Him. As she began to sing, she heard...

"JC, I woke you on that Sunday morning to let you know you had been in the valley long enough and I was moving you to the mountaintop. I was exalting you. Be blessed because I, the great God Jehovah, love you!"

JC thanked God for bringing to remembrance His precious words. She thanked Him for all He had done and given. As she wrote her final message of love for the evening, she heard these words as clearly as one friend stands face-to-face with another: "Move with one purpose in mind. Stand on the mountaintop and shout that I am the great God Jehovah, Elohim, and I love people! Get the vision, write it plainly, and run with the message of My love!"

JC turned to a blank page and began to write her plan to prosper. As she wrote, she placed the titles and at least one goal to be accomplished under each title. Each area of her life: spiritual, physical, financial, emotional, mental, educational, and professional, seemed to tie together. They were interwoven with one thought: standing on the mountaintop and shouting *God loves you*! With all said and done, she vowed to share His message of love with the world and she has done so, since she fell in love with the One who cradles her in His arms and whispers His love for her. She realized there is no end to the goodness of God because He is the good thing—the sure entity, the Entity of all entities, sureness and realness of life—without end!

STEP SEVEN

Write your own plan to prosper!

Jeremiah 29:11 states, "For I know the thoughts I think toward you," says the Lord, "thoughts of peace and not of evil, to give you a future and a hope." Habakkuk 2:2 states, "The Lord answered me, and said, Write the vision, and make it plain on tablets, that he may run who reads it." So the key learning is to let your vision be the guiding tool that supports your dreams.

Take a few minutes to reflect over these three sections to stimulate your thinking.

Word Study: vision, prosper, intervention

1. _____means to be fortunate, to thrive, bloom, or flourish.
2. Having unusual competence in discernment, perception, or foresight is _____.
3. An _____ is the involvement in one's affairs with a divine purpose.

Questions:

1. What is your vision for your life?
2. What steps should be involved to guide your plan?

3. What intervention(s) should you develop to guide your plan?

Tips:

1. Write out a vision for yourself. Search out the components of a vision and build the vision for your future.
2. Pray and seek God's direction as you create steps to fulfilling your vision.
3. Move into your destiny based on your vision.

Milton Keynes UK
Ingram Content Group UK Ltd.
UKHW020715011223
433473UK00010B/125